Musings Along Life's Journey

Vignettes From The Road

Heidi Honey

@ 2023 Heidi Honey

1st Published by
Zoë Life Christian Communications
www.zoelifebooks.org
2nd Publishing by Amazon KDP

All rights reserved. No part of this book may be produced or transmitted in any form or by any means including, but not limited to, electronic or mechanical, photocopying, recording, or by any information storage and retrieval system without written permission from the publisher, except for the inclusion of brief quotations in a review. All Scripture quotations, unless otherwise indicated, are taken from The New King James Version (NKJV) of the Bible copyright © 1982 by Thomas Nelson, Inc.

Musings Along Life's Journey, Vignettes From The Road

Author: Honey, Heidi
Cover: Heidi Honey and ZLCC
Editor: Heidi Honey and ZLCC

First U.S. Edition
2023 13 Digit
ISBN 978-1

Second U.S. Edition
2023
ISBN: 9798865973737

Soft Cover Perfect Binding. Category:

Personal Memoir
For current information about
releases by Heidi Honey,
www.musingsalonglifesjourney.blog

Printed in the United States of America

Musings Along Life's Journey

Vignettes From The Road

Heidi Honey

In Memoria

To begin this second printing of Musings Along Life's Journey, I want to share a few thoughts about my dear sister in the Lord, Sabrina Adams, who was my publisher for the first edition. I have the distinction of authoring the final book published by Sabrina, just before she lost her battle with cancer.

Sabrina would call me "Dear Heart" when we spoke on the phone, and she became my own Dear Heart as we worked on the editing and all the other work it took to publish this, my first book. She got me from manuscript to nights of editing together, gently prompting me to write the pieces that she needed to publish this book in the first place. I was honored that she included my name with hers in the Cover & Editor section. As we worked, we shared our families with each other, and I am saddened that I didn't get the chance to meet Sabrina, her husband Brian, daughter Eliya, daughter Brittany & her husband and daughters. Thank you to Brian for permission to republish with Amazon.

Sabrina fought the good fight, fulfilling her promise to Father God by founding Zoe Life Christian Communications, getting Christian writers published, as long as she had breath. All for God's glory!

Dedication

First, I dedicate this book to Father God, who inspires my writing by the Holy Spirit, and Jesus Christ who saved me.

Second, I dedicate this to my loving husband John, for all the grace he gave me and his patience through my writing and this publishing journey. My husband has grown into the most loving, caring, giving, and compassionate man I know. I thank God each day for the great gift He's given me in my husband John.

Third, but definitely not least, I dedicate this work of love to my children and their families God has blessed us with. My daughter Eliza and her husband Christopher and children Jackson Douglas & Rosemary Elizabeth Sheppard, my son Christopher and his wife Jennifer and children Nataleigh Elizabeth & Ashlynn Hope Honey, my son Harold and his wife Jana and children Owen Patrick & Logan James Honey, and my son Alexander and his wife Joanna and their children Caleb John, Faith Marie, and Steven Michael Honey. There would not be any stories to write if not for my family and those they connected me with. My prayer is that all these precious souls will walk in the ways of the Lord and fulfill His plans for them on this earth. May God be glorified in all that follows.

Table of Contents

Introduction 11

Boxes of Time 13
My Son, Be Wise 15
Times and Other Times 19
2018 21
2019 25
2020 27
2021 28
2022 33
My Interest in Communion 39
My Healing Journey 47
With Every Heartbeat 54
The Healing Journey Continues 56
The Adventure Begins! 65
He Has Gone Before Me 80
Becoming as a Child 85
Jewish Thoughts 94
My Supernatural Experience 107
The Spirit of Poverty 118
With A Voice of Singing 129
Yellow Bananas 135

Conclusion 142
Author, Heidi Honey 146

Introduction

When I was born, fourth child and second daughter to my parents, Harry & Ellen Stahl, the nurse said, "That's such a beautiful baby, she needs a name," a couple days after my birth. Thus my given name, Heidi Ellen Stahl, came to be. Two meanings of Heidi are: battle maiden and princess. Ellen, which means shining light, was my mother's name, and Stahl in German means steel. When I was eighteen, my husband John added Honey to my name when we wed. I don't think my parents realized the portent in the names I received, but I love to find name meanings, which is why I included my grand- children's middle names in the dedication. So here goes: I am a battle maiden princess, a shining light, hard as steel, and sweet as honey.

As of this printing, I have been married to John for forty-one years, blessed with four children and their spouses, and nine grandchildren. John and I have "retired" to Henderson, New York. I put retired in quotes because I have never stopped working odd jobs and my husband always has a project -or six- in the works. I am an editor, blogger, caregiver, an ordinary woman made extraordinary by the power that resides within me since I accepted Jesus Christ as my savior, becoming a Christian.

Musings Along Life's Journey
By Heidi Honey

This is my first book, based on my blog that can be found at: www.musingsalonglifesjourney.blog Join me as I share my musings and adventures, vignettes of my journey over nearly six decades of life on this earth. I pray that my testimonies encourage you and stimulate your desire to taste and see that the Lord is good, giving thanks to the Father and glory to the Son.

Boxes of Time

One day I was looking at a calendar and realizing how we put our days into tidy little boxes. We plan months and even years before the days arrive. We want to know what to expect as far ahead as possible, when none of this time is promised to us. The Lord tells us all our days are in His hands; none of us is promised another day, but we assume we will have many more. Have you noticed how far ahead we plan and how sure of ourselves we are as we schedule and plan?

We schedule doctor appointments three months, six months—even twelve months ahead; dentist visits six months or a year ahead, yearly physicals, and many more medical appointments, depending on age or how many people you're responsible for. These all get put into our calendar boxes. If you are a teacher, you need at least an outline for 180 days of classroom lessons, scheduled around standardized testing dates, vacations and holidays. We can have weekly, monthly, quarterly, yearly schedules, as well as five- and ten-year predictions. With children there's nursery school, preschool, elementary, middle and high school, then college. You get a job after college, then start projecting your path toward retirement; there is usually a wedding and house hunting thrown in.

Musings Along Life's Journey
By Heidi Honey

In our house, we have a calendar full of family birthdays and anniversaries, small group meetings and a cleaning job twice a week, three Thursdays a month for my local Stonecroft group activities jotted down, monthly Book Club and Garden Club, then church appointments...what a busy life we plan! But what does God say about all this?

My Son, Be Wise

"Do not boast about tomorrow, For you do not know what a day may bring forth." (Proverbs 27:1)

J ames Chapter 4:13-16 says, Do not Boast About Tomorrow.

Come now, you who say, "Today or tomorrow we will go to such and such a city, spend a year there, buy and sell, and make a profit". whereas you do not know what will happen tomorrow. For what is your life? It is even a vapor that appears for a little time and then vanishes away. Instead you ought to say, "If the Lord wills, we shall live and do this or that." But now you boast in your arrogance. All such boasting is evil."

We worry endlessly about what might never come. We can't put God in a box and expect Him to follow our instructions. How much time do you spend filling the calendar boxes with your busy schedule, not thinking to ask God about what He might have in store? The verses above are just two of many

Musings Along Life's Journey
By Heidi Honey

Scriptures where the Lord reminds us, we are not in charge of the days of our lives. Here's another one:

A man's heart plans his way. But the LORD directs his steps. (Proverbs 16:9)

How much time have you spent planning and worrying about things that never occur, or don't happen as you thought? I spent my high school years riding home with my mom from visits with my father's parents at their trailer. She worried endlessly about what she was going to do with the folks when they couldn't live alone. Turned out Mom retired and moved away before that time came. My grandparents lived with my family and I took care of them until they died. Mom was able to assist in many ways from where she lived and visited frequently. A few months after Grandma died, she stopped to visit Grandpa on her way to our house, at his trailer. He had returned to the trailer and wasn't managing well, his pipes had frozen and he'd not gotten out to get groceries. She was able to convince him to come back to live with us for the remainder of his life.

I like to make notes of what I'm hearing on scraps of paper as I go about my daily life. Today as I gathered them, transferring them into my notebook, I found a common theme:

Perspective. Included in these notes is dying to self; It's not about me! This includes deepening my relationship with the Lord, growing deeper in God's love expressed in Christ Jesus:

Be Wise, My Son

*God so loved the world that He gave His only begotten Son,
that whoever believes in Him should not perish but have everlasting life.
For God did not send His Son into the world to condemn the world,
but that the world through Him might be saved.*
(John 3:16-17)

Perspective

From God's perspective, 2 Peter 3:8 tells us: ... beloved, do not forget this one thing, that with the Lord one day is as a thousand years, and a thousand years as one day.

It's not about me, my glory, fame, concerns or schedule; it's all about God's plans for our lives and how we fit into them. I pray we all come into deeper communion with the God of the Universe, Who made us and chose to live in and through us in Jesus Christ.

*Therefore do not be like them [the hypocrites]. For your Father knows the things you have need of before you ask Him.
In this manner, therefore, pray: Our Father in heaven, Hallowed be Your name.
Your kingdom come. Your will be done
On earth as it is in heaven.*

(Matthew 6:8-10)

Did you know God can't give you grace for tomorrow because it's not here yet? So let the calendar hold your dates, but remember to make room for God's Will, not your own.

Times and Other Times

Devotions look different in different seasons.

One day I was replying to a young woman's blog post talking about finding time to connect with the Lord. Here's what I replied to her: "I appreciate your words, especially coming from a busy wife with young children and a job. I'm past that point, but still can struggle having concentrated time with the Lord each day. Part of it is a lack of developing discipline. I am much closer in my relationship with God now than I used to be. By the time I actually met Jesus, I was 20 and a mother of 2 children with a third on the way. I had not been raised reading the Bible and praying each day, so I was not sure how to do time devoted to the Lord. At that time, if I could do a 15-minute devotional book each day, I was doing a stellar job when I was raising my children. I resorted to listening to a lot of Scripture songs and Christian radio. I learned a lot of Scriptures from my children's cassettes and the Worship songs we did in church. Kind of thin feedings, (kind of like the boxed mac & cheese I swore I'd never feed my own children!) but that's what I could wrap my mind around at that point. I believe the best thing you can do is seek the Lord and ask the Holy Spirit to show you what's right for you today!"

2018

At the point I was responding to her, it was 2018 and I was doing a rather complicated daily routine. I had the time since my husband was away working on the house in Lowville while I was in Henderson. Having purchased **The Gaither Homecoming Bible**, I began reading Genesis and Galatians daily, a chapter or two each day, along with the hymns and devotional thoughts scattered through the pages. Hearing how good it is to take daily communion from several different sources, I began doing that also.

So this was my routine:
- Communion
- Genesis and Galatians plus devotionals included on the pages
- **The Healing Scriptures** by Sid Roth [free download @ www.sidroth.org]
- **Names of Christ** edited & introduced by James S. Bell, Jr.
- **The Power of the Blood of Jesus** by Andrew Murray
- **Draw Me Close to You, Integrity Devotions** by Greg Asimakopoulos [songs found on YouTube].

Here is what a morning at that time looked like: So, I sit for communion in my quiet place with my shot glass of watered-down grape juice. [I've learned wine in the Bible was the fresh crushed grapes boiled down and diluted 20/1 with water; in Ukraine they make a similar fruit drink they call Compote these days] and my thin rice cake. [I don't do gluten, but that's another topic] my notebook

Musings Along Life's Journey
By Heidi Honey

with pen, reading glasses, Bible and books listed above. I keep a shawl I crocheted handy in case it's
cool.

    Once seated, I give thanks to the Lord, then read and contemplate one name of Christ and one page of **The Healing Scriptures**. Following the accounts in Matthew 26:26-30, Mark 14:22-26, Luke 22:15-20,
and 1 Corinthians 11:23-25, I take the bread and give thanks to God and remember this is Christ's body broken for me and for the nations. I read one thought in **The Power of The Blood of Jesus** and take the cup, which is reminding me of the new covenant—Jew and Gentile becoming one new man, the 39 stripes Jesus took for my healing; every disease, illness, and infirmity category covered. Also, complete covering for sin [animal blood had to be reapplied frequently] and the bringing together of the Church body. After giving thanks, I take and drink. Then as they did at

the Last Supper, I sing the song for the day [I've found most of them on YouTube; they're older songs] and read the short devotion and prayer at the end from **Draw Me Close to You**. Depending on the day, I may stay in my quiet place for a bit more.

At this point in time I didn't read long passages in my Bible. I aimed to spend extended times in my quiet place a couple times a week to seek the Lord
in a deeper way and/or soak in worship. I also got a lot of teachings from Sid Roth's ministry guests and still do today.

Abba Father

My word for this year was Abba Father, where I endeavored to grow closer to Father God; realizing I have a loving heavenly Dad. Also seeking deeper understanding of healing as well as other things of God.

I ended these thoughts in 2018 like this:
So, at this point in my life, it's much different than any other in my adult life has been. We are empty nesters and my husband is away several days each week. In some ways, it's more challenging because some days I can busy myself with odd things and not do my 'normal' routine. I have determined not to take condemnation if I don't get the whole routine in or if I end up doing it at a different time of day. Once in a while-usually when we're

traveling- I don't get a real quiet time. Often, one or all of my devotional books come with me and I read on the way what I can. I know Father is with me always, so I strive to take this time to remind me of that fact.

2019

I n 2019 my word for the year was Shalom.

Shalom is a blessing encompassing all of life and living.

The notes on page 1785 in the **One New Man Bible** state: Shalom comes from Shalem meaning to be complete. When there is Shalom, there is tranquility, justice, sufficient food, clothing, housing. It is also a declaration of war, contending for these things to manifest in our lives. There is Divine health, with no sickness.

Shalom means an absence of: disorder, injustice, bribery, corruption, conflict, lack,
hatred, abuse, violence, pain, suffering, immorality, and all other negative forces.
In other words, Shalom means: Psalm 84:11,

"For the LORD God is a sun and shield; The LORD will give grace and glory;
No good thing will He withhold from those who walk uprightly.

So in 2019 I learned a lot about what we have in Jesus and what is awaiting us in heaven. As Believers, heaven is not just what is to come, it's also Jesus living inside; the fullness of God and the Holy Spirit meaning heaven on earth when we grasp the meaning of God being Abba Father, and Shalom being our

Musings Along Life's Journey
By Heidi Honey

por
tio
n.

This year I used the **Moravian Daily Texts**. My sister lived in Charlotte, NC where she attended a Moravian church and got me started on the Daily Texts several years ago. I stopped after two years because I wanted to read more of the Bible than the short passages, hymn portion and devotion they use. In 2019, I decided to try them again for accountability. I also got the workbook for **Psalm 91**, *God's Shield Of Protection* by Peggy Joyce Ruth and worked through the book and workbook. It was good background for this time we're in during the 2020 "pandemic" as so many people are reading and declaring this Psalm several times a day.

Later in 2019 I attended a seminar at our church with Dr. Mark Virkler based on his book **4 Keys to Hearing God's Voice**. As I started reading the book by Mark & Patti Virkler and practicing two-way journaling, the **Moravian Daily Texts** and Psalm 91 study fell by the wayside that fall. It was all good though! The Lord was really speaking encouragement through the journaling and I began watching Kevin Zadai's **Warrior Notes** videos on YouTube.

2020

My word for this year is Emmanuel, *God with us.* I have begun using, **Rose Petals**, *A Devotional* by Rose Reggiacorte Sieber. I have had this book since proofreading it in 2016 for Cheryl, head of Olive Press Publisher and decided it was high time I used it! Each day I take my "Leave Your Fears Behind" journal and **Rose Petals** book and write the day, date and time in one corner, **Rose Petals** at the top. I also note special events above Rose Petals, then write the Scriptures for the day, often personalizing them. Next, I write down what the Lord had spoken to Rose, personalizing and highlighting what speaks to me. On what is left of the journal page I write my thanks and praise, often repentance and prayer. I brought my journal to our small group one evening to share a page, and my leader Peggy pointed out an empty space on the page, so I have started doodling around what I write down or writing more of what the Spirit is prompting. Now I understand how my Crossroads Prison Ministry students fill up the spaces in their lessons! I have been taking communion frequently, but not every day. When our church did a 21 day fast in January, I started using a one-hour timer on my phone and sitting in my quite place for an hour with my two-way journal and planning pad. I endeavor to spend most of the hour praying/singing in tongues. I have done this once or twice a week and am seeing good fruit from it!

2021

This year has been different from the start. One Sunday morning in December, I came into the pre-service prayer meeting with two Scriptures colliding in my head: from Him, through Him, to Him are all things, He who began a good work will be faithful to complete it...which I shared and encouraged Pastor Josh with. I have learned most scripture from songs; many taken from various translations, so here is the New King James version:

> *"For of Him and through Him and to Him are all things, to whom be glory forever. Amen."* (Romans 11:36)

> *"...being confident of this very thing, that He who has begun a good work in you will complete it until the day of Jesus Christ..."* (Philippians 1:6)

Not only did this year start differently due to COVID-19 dragging on and the new vaccine coming out, but the presidential office is also unsettled. This year my devotional life is also different. I am working my way through some of the books I have acquired, going day-by-day through them so I can

absorb more. I began a new journal on the

first of January to keep track of what I am studying and learning.

On January 1, I also began the annual twenty-one day fast with our congregation.

Musings Along Life's Journey
By Heidi Honey

Pastor Paul was doing a YouVersion study on the book of John. I don't have the YouVersion Bible app on my phone, but realized there are twenty-one chapters in John. My sister-in-law gave me a nice calendar journal for Christmas, so I opened it to the first of January and began fasting and concentrating on one chapter of the book of John each day. I would read that day's chapter through on my **New Living Translation (NLT) Bible** on my phone before rising in the morning, then use my **One New Man Bible** to read again and journal what I was discovering later in the day.

I have not been reading or watching news reports, but I'm not sticking my head in the sand or totally uninformed. Not a day goes by that someone doesn't fill me in on news about the federal offices or COVID-19. I listened to podcasts from Shawn Bolz' Exploring series, Bethel Sermons and Kris Vallotton. I also began watching Elijah Streams on YouTube, where Steve Shultz interviews prophets and seers to see what God's perspective on things is. He interviews Kat Kerr each Wednesday discussing what Heaven is saying about the presidential election. Others I've watched are Robin D. Bullock, who has been having dreams and visions of President Donald J. Trump since 2014, Manuel Johnson, who had a vison of 2022 with no one wearing masks, and more people sharing encouraging prophecies from God's perspective. I'm excited about what the

Lord is doing to expose the darkness and make room for His glory to manifest in a big way. It's not just about the USA, but countries and governments around the world!

2021

For the first time since I began, I took a three week break from my weekly blog while fasting. Not
that I didn't have anything to say, but I had so much coming into my life from the Bible study, blogs, YouTube and books I was reading that I couldn't settle on one topic for a post. I also connected with a Pastor with a ministry in Kenya who has been mentoring me through Zoom meetings once a week. We are studying the Communion With God (CWG) materials [Dr. Mark Virkler]; he was given a scholarship to CWG's school and his mission is to disciple others so they can disciple others, to spread the truth of what it is to have the fullness of God within and be able to hear the Lord speak. What a marvelous time we live in that we can connect halfway around the world in ministry, face to face (virtually)!

To follow up my twenty-one days of John, I began a 90-day book **Exploring the Prophetic**, by Shawn Bolz on January 22nd. This is part of his ministry, mentoring people in the prophetic and in hearing God's voice. It has been a good concentration for me at this point in my walk, along with the weekly CWG classes Brother Cyprien is leading me in. From Truth For Life, I ordered **An Ocean of Grace**, *A Journey to Easter with Great Voices from the Past* by Tim Chester, a Lenten devotional. It arrived with a second copy of the book so I gave one to my Life Group leader, who is enjoying going through it daily with me. With all this going on, it was mid- February before I determined my word for the year was actually a couplet of Scriptures, as noted above, and I revealed it in my blog post on February 18th. Ever of Scriptures with Pastor,

Musings Along Life's Journey
By Heidi Honey

since the December morning I shared that couplet it has stuck in my mind and spirit. This word from the Lord to me has become extremely pertinent and comforting as I walk through this year.

2022

My word for the year 2022 is *forgiveness*. I began with **The Prophet's Devotional**, *365 Daily Invitations To Hear, Discern, And Activate The Prophetic* by Jennifer LeClaire for my basic devotions and added shorter devotion books to read along with it. I began reading through Ephesians, Philippians and Colossians in The Passion Translation, spending ten minutes singing to the Lord after ten minutes of speaking in tongues. I did this through March and found fruit and understanding on the Church and unity. What follows are the other books I've worked through.

    Stories From The Glory by Dr. Kevin L. Zadai with Ruth Carneal, which encouraged me to seek the glory by seeking the Lord. After that I began **Preparations For A Move Of God In Your Life** by Sandra G. Kennedy—which was interrupted by [I gave it to a sister younger in the faith], **Heaven,** *An Unexpected Journey by* Jim Woodford with Thom Gardner which encouraged me to live in the present and take the forgiveness Jesus has for us to give others. I followed these with **The Thrill of Victory, The Agony of Defeat** by Randy Clark in which I learned to keep praying and declaring healing over people. Randy said 200 times may go by before you see someone healed, but you'll never lose the hunger to pray after that!

Next was **Divine Opportunity,** *Finding God in the Conversations of Everyday Life,* by Ryan Montague, PhD which was interrupted [I sent it in a box to Love Packages] by **60 Day Healing Devotional,** *Encountering Your Path To Healing* by

Musings Along Life's Journey
By Heidi Honey

Dr. Kevin L. Zadai, which encouraged me to claim healing and pull it down from heaven. Then I read **The Joy of Intercession,** *40 Day Encounter* by Beni Johnson, whose joy is more catching than the common cold! Oh, I was blessed to be reading **The Power of Communion,** *Accessing Miracles Through the Body and Blood of Jesus,* by Beni Johnson with Bill Johnson when she went on to glory a short time ago due to cancer.

In October, I began **Walking in the Miraculous**, *A 30 Day Devotional*, by Chad Gonzales, followed by **Think Like Jesus**, *40 Days to Creating a Miracle Mindset*, also by Chad Gonzales which emphasized what we have and who we are in Christ. This year I have taken the fetters off and chosen not to stress if I miss a day—or three—of my devotional readings and it's the first year I can remember that I have not quit a 365-day devotional between July and August! I began the year closing my office door for 30-45 minutes, doing my devotional time and soaking. This did not please my husband because I was shutting him out. So, I ended up keeping my devo books in the living room. I do these either as part of my morning routine, take them if we're on the road that day, or read them later in the day. I may do part of it earlier and the rest later. Some days I only get through, **The Prophet's Devotional.**

So, what does this all have to do with the word for the year: Forgiveness? Through it all, the Spirit keeps reminding me of things and people I need to forgive. Some of them I know I've forgiven before,

2022

but I am learning to be obedient to the prompts, leading to deeper facets of forgiveness.

When Andrew and John Eastmond came to minister in our church on September 4, 2022, the Lord reaffirmed my calling to forgiveness. Here is what the Spirit spoke over me from Andrew's lips:

Word from Andrew Eastmond Sep 4, 2022

The Lord wants to restore what was stolen, what was robbed, killed and destroyed, and this the coolest journey she's ever been on because it's not costing her everything like it used to.

No, she's receiving abundance every day to function. It's not her strength, it's Christ in her giving strength, Christ in her—this is an amazing journey she's on. It's awesome. Thank You Father. Halleluia. Lord, I pray the same thing for her as when blind Bartimaeus was down, he wanted to get with Jesus and people criticized him and told him to shut up. People are so cruel. They're so unreasonable. They just show how ungodly they are, and it hurts, and I'm not trying to underestimate how much it hurts you, you know more about it than I do. It really does hurt and Father, I ask You to heal her and soothe her wounds. We need to come to the place to forgive people that hurt us. We need to come to the place and forgive as much as we can and leave it with God because if we don't come to the place where we can pray for them, they're probably going to be doomed.

Musings Along Life's Journey
By Heidi Honey

I always see people that are unkind or rude, I say Father, If I don't pray for them, even if they've insulted me, and they answer for what they did, they're doomed and I don't want that for them.

You have such a heart for that. God wants to heal you of wounds and offenses. I thank you Father for soothing. Let Him heal you of the wounds and offenses. Father, they haven't got a clue of what they're doing for their futures Father, I thank You that you're doing that in her life (www.andreweastmond.com).

So, we need to quickly forgive those who offend us and not take offenses into our heart to fester. Jesus said, "Father forgive them for they know not what they're doing." The Spirit of God is revealing it goes deeper and farther than we thought. Not just forgive them for what they're doing because they may know, but forgive them because they don't know how their words or actions will affect those they are offending in the long term. Those who have seen hell confirm what the Bible says, you don't want even your worst enemy to go there, totally separated from the light, love and presence of God and eternally tortured in dark places! Let the love of God so completely overwhelm you that no unforgiveness can remain in your heart and ask the Lord to clear your mind as well.

2022

As I end telling you about my devotionals, I want to reiterate my first thought: devotions look different in different seasons. These days you can easily find a daily devotional on-line or on a Bible app that will remind you each day. Most of these take fifteen minutes or less. If you have a devotional or study Bible, it will have a daily reading plan. I don't recommend going through the Bible in a year unless you just want a broad overview. A two-year plan is usually easier.

Boiling down the purpose of devotional time, it is time spent in fellowship with the Father, the Son, and the Holy Spirit of God. Reading the Bible and digesting other's thoughts is a start, but He wants your heart. I take a bit of time when I'm settling in to bed, before I rise in the morning, and in the
"night seasons" when I'm awakened, to just rest in the arms of the Father, thanking Him for being there and for all He's doing in my life. As I say, it's a resting in His presence. Maybe your time, like mine, is while you are driving. I've stopped listening to the radio most times when I drive and find it's more time to talk with Him. I hope these thoughts spur you to find creative ways to get the Word of God and the communion with the Spirit going.

My Interest in Communion

I have gained more interest in communion as my years as a Believer have gone by. I want to share some things I've gleaned along this particular journey. I recommend a book I proofread in 2020, part of [Messianic] Rabbi Jim Appel's, Appointed Times Series **Khag Pesakh, Passover.** He sheds light on the original Passover and what Jesus revealed as He celebrated Passover with his disciples the night He was betrayed and instituted what we call Communion today.

Communion

Lil deFin, great granddaughter of Smith Wiggles- worth, says he took daily communion to remind himself of the "Great Exchange" Jesus' life for his. Other people have found healing or spiritual growth. I just gained realization that Jesus' Blood is still poured out on the mercy seat and the scars from the nails are still in His heavenly body. I see it as part of beginning to understand the One who was and is and is to come, as our Lord is called in the book of Revelation verses 1:4, 1:8, 4:8, and 11:17. In other words, Jesus is the Lamb who was slain before the foundations of the world, so His Blood has been poured out since then. All impossible to understand with our human minds; I'm so glad the Holy Spirit is such a good teacher!

Musings Along Life's Journey
By Heidi Honey

Have you ever taken communion in your own home? Traditionalists believe you need to be an ordained minister or lay leader to administer the communion elements, but we are kings and priests in Christ Jesus, so I think it's okay to do this. I don't think the Lord cares if we don't use matza and wine. When I was a youth, an older friend led us in communion with Kool-Aid and Ritz crackers. I heard Dan Mohler on YouTube the other day talking about being at breakfast, having a revelation of Jesus and using a Cheerio out of the bowl for the bread and the milk in the bowl for the wine; if you sense the Lord's presence, whatever you're eating and giving thanks for can be a remembrance of the Lord's table. Let us look at how Jesus began this sacrament.

Institution of the Lord's Supper

For I received from the Lord that which I also delivered to you: that the Lord Jesus on the same night in which He was betrayed took bread; and when He had given thanks, He broke it and said, "Take, eat; this is My body which is broken for you; do this in remembrance of Me." In the same manner He also took the cup after supper, saying, "This cup is the new

*covenant in My blood. This do, as often as you drink it, in remembrance of Me."
For as often as you eat this bread and drink this cup, you proclaim the Lord's death till He comes.*
　　　　　(1 Corinthians 11:23-26)

My Interest in Communion

Churches and Christian groups differ in how often to take communion. Some do it every week, some once a month, some only a few special times a year. In our church we have communion the first Sunday of each month. We invite all who profess Jesus as Lord and Savior to partake. When I'm part of a Catholic Mass, I have friends who welcome me there, I know I am not to participate in the sacrament unless I have become a communicant of their church. It is a good thing to know the custom for whichever church you are in when communion comes.

There are those who believe in 'transubstanti- ation': the elements must be taken as the actual body and Blood of Christ and many abide by strict rules about who can administer the elements, where and when. It is one point that has split many congregations. Here is what I found about transub- stantiation in The Oxford Dictionary:

"What does the Bible say about transub- stantiation?
Predominant Passage for Transubstantia- tion. The main passage of Scripture in which Roman Catholics use as a proof text that Transubstantiation occurs is John 6:53-57 where Jesus said to them, "Truly,

truly, I say to you, unless you eat the flesh of the Son of Man and drink his blood, you have no life in you."

Musings Along Life's Journey
By Heidi Honey

If you look at this passage in context, Jesus shocked and offended the religious leaders by saying this. Jewish dietary rules forbid the Israelites from drinking or eating any blood. If you look in a Jewish cookbook, you will find instructions for draining the blood from your meats to make them Kosher. The priests killed and drained the blood of the animal into a ceremonial bowl that was sprinkled on the altar to atone for sins. On Passover they would dip a hyssop branch in the bowl of blood drained from the lamb and sprinkle it on the doorposts and lintel of their home. On the first Passover, the death angel passed over each home with blood on its door, which would have marked the door like the cross of Christ was marked with our Savior's Blood. I note here: the Jewish people have not sacrificed animals since the destruction of Solomon's Temple in A.D. 70.

Churches I have attended have not acknowledge the elements as the actual body and blood. I believe the Lord must reveal this to you as Holy Spirit does with many other mysteries and hard sayings of Jesus. I like what Jonathan Alsop said to his students at the Boston Wine School:

Alsop stresses that his interpretation is subjective. As an example, he cites Christ's offering of bread and wine as his body and blood during the Last Supper.

My Interest in Communion

"*He's saying, spiritually, take me inside you and let my spirit suffuse your spirit, but naturally he does that through these wine and food metaphors,*"

Alsop says. [italics mine] [https://www.npr.org/sections/thesalt/2014/12/25/372727808/what-would-jesus-drink-a-class-exploring-ancient-wines-asks accessed 6-27-2020].

My Interest in Communion

Here are some of the methods for sharing communion elements that I have experienced. For the bread, a loaf of bread is broken in half and each person breaks a piece off, cubes of bread are passed around, crackers, matza or wafers can be used. The
wine or juice can be in communion cups, poured from a pitcher into cups you hold, or in a chalice. The bread and wine can be passed

around or the people go up to the communion table. All can partake at the front or all take it back to their seats. Some dip the bread or wafer into the chalice, take and eat. The leader can lead you when to take the bread and the wine as a group or may tell you to take them as the Spirit leads.

Communion with Billye

I receive Billye Brim's ministry blog posts in my email. On March 27, 2020 she invited her readers to join her for communion in her home, so I grabbed my glass of juice and cracker and clicked on the link in my email to her YouTube video. She explained the following Scriptures which has further added to my understanding of communion. Here is the scripture she used.

Musings Along Life's Journey
By Heidi Honey

Examine Yourself

Therefore whoever eats this bread or drinks this cup of the Lord in an unworthy manner will be guilty of the body and blood of the Lord. But let a man examine himself, and so let him eat of the bread and drink of the cup. For he who eats and drinks in an unworthy manner eats and drinks judgment to himself, not discerning the Lord's body.

For this reason many are weak and sick among you, and many sleep. For if we would judge ourselves, we would not be judged. But when we are judged, we are chastened by the Lord, that we may not be condemned with the world.

(1 Corinthians 11:27-32)

As I understand it, first, we need to discern the Body of Christ, which is the Church, composed of all who are in Christ Jesus. Second, remember the New Covenant in His blood; Jew and Gentile become One New Man. Sid Roth speaks often of this One New Man miracle. When we come to the table of the Lord with unforgiveness toward another or unrepentant, that is when we partake in an unworthy manner.

This leads to the practice of many to take communion daily for healing and divine health. As you see in these Scriptures, if we discern the Body while taking the elements, we will not be weak, sick, or falling asleep in death. It has a lot to do with

My Interest in Communion

forgiveness and repentance. As I take and eat, I
remember what Jesus did and accept His broken body and poured out blood and accept the healing
and completeness in the relationship between

God and His children and His children to each other.

Speaking of elements for communion: I have three shot glasses I found when we were moving which I don't think have ever had wine or liquor in them, but I don't think it matters to the Lord which glass you use. I keep grape juice in the fridge and pour some in the glass, sometimes diluting it with water. In a study of the Biblical meaning for wine, the word "wine" in Hebrew and Greek often refers to non-alcoholic grape juice in the Bible (https:// godsbreath.net/2011/05/20/did-jesus-drink- wine/). So I think it's okay if you dilute wine or even grape juice to have for communion.

Having used several types of crackers, gluten- free matzo, even graham crackers, I take whichever
I have on hand and have also made my own. On Amazon I found you can order a box of the elements with the juice in a cup with a wafer on top, all sealed. Very portable, it keeps for quite some time. I have a friend who leaves a goblet and some kind of bread on a plate for communion on her counter for anyone who comes to be able to partake. She started using grape juice in the cup, but now uses water because the juice sitting out was spoiling.

You can find the words Jesus used with His disciples and the order for the Lord's Supper in these Scriptures:

Musings Along Life's Journey

By Heidi Honey

Matthew 26:26-27
Mark 14:22-23
Luke 22:17-20
1 Corinthians 11:23-26

Pastor Bill Johnson and his wife Beni have some YouTube videos about communion. He takes communion daily not just for his health, but for his entire family. He pleads the blood of Jesus over his children and grandchildren and prays for their healing, and health, and speaks destiny over each one. I have begun this, also praying for my children's marriages as well as my own.

Hallelujah! Our church finally had communion for the first time since the pandemic! We were handed the unit with cup and wafer as we came in and were able to partake as a congregation. I really missed corporate communion. We had a testimony from one of our young mothers. She struggles with an auto-immune disease that's taken away her feeling and some use of parts of her body. She shared with her boss at work, who is also a Christian. Her boss prayed with her and recommended she begin taking daily communion for her healing. She had learned the ritual growing up in church, but never understood what it all meant. Healing! Wholeness! Hope!!!

You can hear her testimony and Pastor Paul Gmitter's sermon on communion: http://www.airportchristian-ellowship.org/sermon-archive/ August 20, 2020 "DO THIS IN REMEMBERANCE OF ME."

My Healing Journey

Genes and Bloodlines

It's a sign of the times: everyone seems to be getting their DNA test done. My husband and son got their DNA tests and then I got mine about a year ago. I put off upgrading to the health report, but recently paid to get it from **23 and Me**. I watched Dr. Francis Myles on **ISN Network** the other day. He was talking about family bloodlines, DNA and sins of the fathers. I've prayed against sins of the past— sins of the fathers—several times over the years and have had some relief from them, but Dr. Myles said that's only part of healing for our past. He said we can symbolically jump the bloodline; choose to denounce our allegiance to our natural lineage and accept the bloodline of Christ in its place.

I followed his directions; finding a red ribbon in my ribbon collection, I placed it across my doorway as they were stretching red ribbons out in the ISN studio. He said to denounce the father's, mother's and husband's blood lines, so I denounced allegiance to the Stahl lineage. Also to the Weinheimer lineage and Honey lineage. Note: I don't "divorce myself from my family; just the things that are not of God." As I jumped the line, I cut off these ties in Jesus' name. There was joy and rejoicing on the other side of the line for me!

I've superimposed the bloodline of Christ over my family lineage and my DNA is changed as of today. I am now part of His generation, open to Christ's destiny. This is a legal transaction in God's courts, teaching which led right into Robert Henderson's

Musings Along Life's Journey

By Heidi Honey

teaching on bringing our case before the courts of Heaven where Christ is our Judge Advocate and Father God our Justice. One thing from his teaching that stuck: if you come to court with your case that's not on the docket because it's already been dealt with, you'll get thrown out for contempt of court. This gave me pause to think how many times I've done this; not believing I have what I ask God for and asking again and again. You can also find Robert Henderson on **It's Supernatural Network (ISN)**.

Eczema

I first had an eczema outbreak on my hands when I had two children in diapers and we moved in the middle of fall, in the chilly, damp winds. When it first broke out, I remembered my Grandma Weinheimer, Mother's mother, had the same malady so I took it as my generational cross to bear. I had nights of intense itching, scaling and bleeding so badly when I was an adult student at the community college that I'd bleed on my papers. Ointments, creams, lotions, Dermatologist, cotton gloves under rubber ones...I was never completely clear that whole period of my life. Thirty-five years into this journey, I had the worst breakout I'd ever had; so severe on the back of my hands that I thought it had turned into something else!

I began hearing testimonies of healing and getting some teaching on what the Bible says about
healing. It dawned on me that stress and unforgiveness

My Healing Journey

can cause many health problems.

We were preparing to spend a month at our daughter's home in Los Angeles and I'd gotten samples of the new eczema ointment from my doctor. It seemed to help, so I asked them to get me a prescription. As we were readying to leave, I found out our health insurance would not approve the medication unless I was examined and found to have eczema over a good portion of my body. I told the doctor I'd wait until I got back. At this same time, I had forgiven my mother and grandmother for anything I'd held against them. I started walking in faith, daily speaking health over my body. I determined to drop the weight of anxious thoughts and vain imaginations. I thanked God He was using this to show me what anxious thought can do and realized it isn't His will in Christ that I continue claiming this malady.

During this time, I also found that all soaps are anti-bacterial from my daughter-in-law, Jana, who studied biology, so I stopped using soaps labeled
anti-bacterial. I also stumbled onto a site that said if water is the first or second ingredient in a cream or lotion, it draws moisture out of your skin instead of keeping it in. Like when you soak in the tub too long and your fingers start to wrinkle; that's the bath water taking water out of your skin. It took a lot of searching, but I finally found a salve that had no water in it. The dermatologist had said I needed to put cream on my hands every time I got them wet. I checked and found even the dermatologist

Musings Along Life's Journey
By Heidi Honey

recommended creams had water as one of their top ingredients.

Well, I came back from that trip to L.A. with
my hands just about healed! A couple months later, I went to show someone my hands and realized I couldn't even see any signs of eczema and she could hardly believe I'd ever

had it! Three years later, my hands are still in excellent condition. I can wash dishes without gloves, work cleaning motel rooms with nytril gloves; no cotton underneath, and use the water-free ointments. This shows me sometimes God heals by showing you how to heal. Praise God from whom all blessings flow!

TMJ

Most people are familiar with TMJ, Temporal Mandibular Joint pain. I used to grind my teeth at night, which may have contributed to my jaw pain. Quite a few years back, I learned to relax my jaw as I was falling asleep and the teeth grinding ceased after a bit. When I started noticing my jaw, I remembered my grandmother's jaw clicking while she was chewing when I heard mine doing the same; I always thought her clicking came from dentures. I talked with our dental hygienist about it and she said, "Sounds like it's lacking lubricant." It was difficult having my mouth opened for dental procedures because my jaw would kind of go out of joint and be painful and need to settle back in. Biting into a larger baby carrot could set it off, as well as other foods. I could feel inflammation.

My Healing Journey

I read that tinnitus, which is another generatonal malady, can be linked to TMJ, so I asked my chiropractor about it. She was excited because she'd heard it also and wanted to try it out. She used her actuator on my jaw. It seemed to help the jaw a bit, but no change in the tinnitus. So I'd tried chiropractor and anti-inflammatory remedies including peanut lavender oil which my chiropractor swears by. The pain, inflammation and clicking weren't there all the time, but came up at irritating and painful intervals.

Sunday March 4th, 2018, my worship team leader prayed in agreement that my jaw was healed. Watching Sid Roth on the ISN app on March 7, 2018, it was about the third time I'd heard Sid had a word of knowledge for healing of jaw and neck. I claimed the healing each time, but on this episode, his guest said, "Open your mouth and let Him work." I did that and felt a cushioning after stretching my jaw. That same evening I watched **The 700 Club** and Pat Robertson had a word of knowledge about pain in someone's jaw, neck, shoulders; intermittent pain...being healed. "You will not need to go to the chiropractor!" I took this as a word from God because I stopped going to the chiropractor almost a year before and was contemplating going back.

I walked in faith, claiming my healing. On March 18, I talked with Shirley, a member of our congregation who has been walking in divine health for over 30 years. She put her hands in mine and perceived I was healed! She imparted a tingling/ burning into my palms and I had tears of great joy! I believe I have healing in my hands when I let it

Musings Along Life's Journey
By Heidi Honey

release by placing my hands on people. I note here that when you have a touch from God, it overwhelms your body and that's why there's tears and great joy. This is two years later. I still stretch my jaw at times just to see it's not painful. If I feel a twinge of discomfort, I don't accept it. I remind familiar spirits I'm healed and don't accept it. It also gives me pause to pray for someone else's jaw. At this point, I sense it's muscles that need to be stretched and not joint; I've had no more clicking and very little discomfort!

Migraine Headaches

Another healing I'd like to share is about migraine headaches. I had my first migraine when I was in Junior High. My doctor put me on a medicine to try to control them; I had them about 3-4 times that year. My father had migraines, so again, it was "inherited". I had more of these headaches as I went through my 20's and 30's. I learned early on when I started seeing the visual effects in one eye, I needed to take aspirin and find a dark place to lie down and sleep it off. If I caught it quick enough, I could head it off and not get a full-blown episode.

We bought some over-the-counter migraine pain reliever and I used it infrequently as needed, with little thought. When I traveled to Bethel Breakouts in Rochester, New York with my worship leader,

Janelle, in October 2017, things came to a head. As we got to the parking area, I suddenly saw the "migraine lights" in my eye. I'd not had a headache for quite some time. I wracked my brain

My Healing Journey

to think of anything I'd eaten or done that would usually trigger the headache, coming up with nothing. My caring leader drove me to the pharmacy to get migraine medicine and I took a dose. The medicine didn't work like it usually does and the episode continued.

That night Havilah Cunnington spoke and when she started praying, she asked for people who had migraine headaches to stand up to be prayed for, then she forcefully prayed against migraines while two friends laid hands on me. I realized then why the headache had come on me that day! Glory to God, I know I no longer have them; I've not even taken acetaminophen since 2017 when this happened, praise God!

With Every Heartbeat

On Monday, April 16, 2018 Sid Roth interviewed Jim Richards. When he started sharing how science is confirming what the Bible says, my ears perked up. I was introduced to Dr. Caroline Leaf several years ago, who also talks about the body, thoughts, and God's Word being confirmed. Jim said Scientists have found that words are of different frequencies and every organ in our body has its own frequency. When we hold onto hurts, offenses and unforgiveness, it becomes a vibration that hurts our body. If we forgive and confess God's thoughts and blessings, it sends healing frequencies through our body.

> *I beseech you therefore, brethren, by the mercies of God, that you present your bodies a living sacrifice, holy, acceptable to God, which is your reasonable service.*

And do not be conformed to this world, but be transformed by the renewing of your mind, that you may prove what is that good and acceptable and perfect will of God.
(Romans 12:1-2)

Musings Along Life's Journey
By Heidi Honey

Jim also said science has found every cell in your body is reprogrammed every time your heart beats. The heart reprograms the cells to what you are thinking. This means if I'm upset about what I saw on the news or the person who cut me off in traffic, I take on thoughts that are detrimental to my well-being. If I replace those thoughts with words of love, promises of God and who I am in Christ, I create positive, healthy words for my body to feed on. That makes this proverb come alive:

A merry heart does good, like medicine, But a broken spirit dries the bones.
(Proverbs 17:22)

Dr. Caroline Leaf, a brain specialist, concurs with all this. She gives the illustration of two trees: one black and dying and the other green and thriving. She equates these with bad thoughts and good thoughts. I've heard a lot about healing and thought life lately and noticed some things. Many people testify they are healed of arthritis when they choose to forgive people that they were holding in bondage by their judgments against them. Many illnesses are exacerbated by the stress of worry, fear, depression. I believe these things have contributed to every malady I have.

Dr. Mark Virkler talks about cellular memory. He says any trauma to your body is held in your cellular memory. We need to release our cells from past trauma to set our bodies free.

The Healing Journey Continues

I'm not saying I've yet obtained complete Divine health, but I'm well on my way. This is a journey I'm walking with the Spirit of God as my guide. I pray, "Father, let Your will be done on Earth as it is in Heaven." In Heaven there's no sickness or infirmity. There are no anxious thoughts, grudges held or offenses taken and no bitterness. All of Heaven is filled with the great love of God and complete Shalom! With this, let's talk about walking in love.

> *And above all things have fervent love for one another, for "love will cover a multitude of sins."*
> (1 Peter 4:8)

This means choosing not to hold on to offenses or slandering people. Things done without love fester inside our beings and lead to all kinds of physical and mental dis-ease. There is a choice: am I going to use this situation in my life to be bitter or better?

Bitterness and unforgiveness are good food for cancer, arthritis, heart disease, mental

Musings Along Life's Journey
By Heidi Honey

illness, and many other things we suffer with; can anyone say "fibromyalgia"? The couple who lead our local Healing Rooms said every person that's come in with fibromyalgia has left healed! Am I going to lay down and accept the history of diseases that do not come from our loving Heavenly Father?

> *The thief does not come except to steal, and to kill, and to destroy.*
> *I have come that they may have life, and that they may have it more abundantly.*
> (John 10:10)

I'm truly realizing I can't blame God for any of these things my body has. If it's bad: stealing, killing, destroying, it comes from the devil. He's been a liar since the beginning and all the demons back this up. We invite familiar spirits which often come from our parents or other ancestors, especially when we take things as our "cross to bear". Pastor Bill Johnson says, "God = good ALL the time; devil = bad ALL the time" and has everyone repeat it several times. In other words, one of the great lies we believe is God uses sickness to teach us or increase our humility… faith…if God is good, why would He put sickness on us? Jesus paid for our healing completely with what He suffered.

Some people say witches heal. Well, if the devil put sickness on you, couldn't he take it off you through his servants? The liar doesn't change his

The Healing Journey Continues

tactics: doing poor copies of Jesus' miracles that deceive many. Familiar spirits or demons don't go willingly, you have to break your agreement with them.

Here are some of satan's lies I've heard; many about God's Chosen people.

1. Jews use Christian blood sacrifice to make their matzos or drink the blood of child sacrifice. TRUTH: Remember what I said about the Jews in Jesus' day being offended by Him saying, "You must drink My blood and eat My flesh or you will have no part in Me."? If they made sure the meat was bled out, why would they put blood in?

2. The Jews have been replaced by the Church as God's favored people; "Replacement Doctrine". TRUTH: You only need to read the book of Romans to see how the Jew was turned away for a "short time" until the fullness of the Gentiles came in. These days, The Spirit is drawing many Jews to repent and

accept Yeshuah as their Messiah!

3. Jews caused the bubonic plague. TRUTH: the dietary and cleanliness laws God gave through Moses kept them from getting the disease.

4. My husband decided I didn't love him and maybe I was having an affair with my Pastor. TRUTH: My pastor wouldn't meet with me without someone else around so there'd be

Musings Along Life's Journey
By Heidi Honey

5. no semblance of evil. I made my care group leader nervous one evening when I stood around until I knew I could sit without being next to a man!

6. How could a loving God send anyone to hell? TRUTH: God didn't create hell for people, but for satan, fallen angels and demons. Hell is total separation from God; He sent Jesus to die to reunite us with Father God; close the separation. So, God doesn't send anyone to hell. It's our choice to accept or reject Jesus's gift of salvation, the only remedy for sin. We won't be able to blame anyone else for our failure to accept salvation either!

Satan's lies never really change; they just look a bit different. No matter how many times

Apologists have answered all the standard questions, each generation has more people who believe the lies and ask the time-worn questions. The devil is so lacking in creativity, how do we fall into his plans so easily?

    I still have tinnitus, which is another family malady. I went to an ear, nose and throat doctor who tried everything short of surgery to correct it. Remember my chiropractor tried also? I have released my cellular memory from the trauma of loud things I have subjected them to and wear earmuffs or plugs most of the time now. Did you know tinnitus is not actually in your ears? It's your brain attempting to cover/counteract loud sounds. I've agreed I'm healed, had hands laid on me, been

The Healing Journey Continues

anointed with oil, but the ringing continues. I like what Dr. Mark Virkler says: "I am healed, and the symptoms are disappearing." Another thing I've learned to declare is: "My body is a well-watered garden and in a well-watered garden there is no lack" which means I am healed and complete in Jesus' name. I declare healing and health over myself and pray the Lord's will be done daily. I have chosen to renounce family blood lines and curses. I press on, pursuing the abundant life in Christ that God offers us. I proclaim Jesus is my healer and I am growing in Him and moving toward divine health.

I claim often:

*The LORD will guide you
continually, And satisfy your
soul in drought, And
strengthen your bones;
You shall be like a watered garden,
And like a spring of water, whose waters
do not fail.*
(Isaiah 58:11)

Major Changes

My mother was a Home Economics teacher (now called Home and Careers) and at home, she taught us a lot about foods and health. My dad never drank milk, but always had orange juice mixed with lemonade. Mom kept Archway cookies in the house, and we had ice cream for dessert almost every night after a meat and potatoes meal to satisfy him. Mom always made a tossed salad and had at least one other vegetable on the table every night,

Musings Along Life's Journey

By Heidi Honey

to encourage the healthy part of the meal. Dad was a smoker, a bit overweight and had high blood pressure and cholesterol. He died of massive heart failure at 46 years old. He'd stopped smoking just a year before and was feeling much better than he had.

We children grew up with a mixture of semi-healthy and semi-lazy eating. Canned soups and spaghetti or pork & beans out of cans were our lunches for non-school days, breakfasts were usually oatmeal; Mom would cook it on the stove, or we'd have packets of instant. We also had our share of sweet cold cereals. Overweight and underweight ran in the family as well as heart problems, arthritis...I'd say we were a fairly typical family in the 1960's to 80's.

When my children were young, we continued the instant oatmeal, eggs occasionally, the odd pancakes or waffles with bacon or sausage. We had a lot of "healthy" boxed cereal approved by the WIC [Women Infants & Children] program having 14 grams of sugar or less per serving. There was always either apple, grape, or a mix of the two juices, which I watered down, as well as a cup of milk. We ate a lot of peanut butter and jelly sandwiches, tuna salad, or boxed mac & cheese with an apple or carrots and milk for lunch. Supper had a lot of pastas and other starches, made a little healthier with meat from John's hunting and fishing. At one point, corn was the only vegetable the whole family would eat! I used to bake when I got bored, so we had a lot of

The Healing Journey Continues

cookies, muffins, brownies and pie. I gained the

"typical" ten pounds each decade.

The 'C' word?

When I found I had breast cancer August 31, 2010, I'd been on hormone pills for ten years to regulate my periods. I frequently took pain relievers and had been on a daily diuretic for at least ten years, and I was also on allergy medicine daily for three years. I was asking the Lord why I was taking these medications and when and how I could get off them.

That evening when my surgeon called to tell me my diagnosis, the Spirit had whispered to me before she told me, so I was ready for it. My mom had breast cancer that went to her uterus, dying at 74
years old, but the Lord kept me from fear. Doc said it was so small a mass that it was category 1; not even stage 1. Oh, and there were two tiny lumps, so close together she couldn't remove one without the other. By the time we were done talking, we were chuckling. That's God's grace! Grace continued when she called right back after hanging up, "Oh, it's estrogen receptive so stop the hormone pills." Tick one medication off my list! Of course, after the surgery and radiation I was on an estrogen blocker for 5 years, but off the hormone pills.

At that time, there was a lot of healing going on in our congregation, but I didn't sense God wanting to instantly heal me. I just wanted surgery done soon enough so I could go on my planned trip to Israel that October. I was reading a big book about Israel

Musings Along Life's Journey
By Heidi Honey

in preparation for my trip, which I carried around to my appointments. I had many opportunities to share with people some things of God and about Israeli history. I realize now sometimes His healing is a journey that includes doctors and medications. Sid Roth says a miracle is instantaneous; progressive improvement is called healing. Think about Lazarus being in the grave for 4 days before Jesus came, to show God's glory. My friend and I pondered how God would get glory from someone being gradually healed; so people could discount God doing the healing. We decided we need to trust God to know how to bring glory to Himself through these things.

Dieting?

Fast forward to February of 2015. I had been working out at **Curves for Women** three times a week for several years, but I'd crept up to my highest weight of 172 pounds. At the same time, I was working at **Dunkin' Donuts** across the parking lot from **Curves** and eating our products. I got the **Curves Fitness & Weight Management Plan** book. With the high protein plan, I was eating a lot of hard-boiled eggs and string cheese which raised my LDL cholesterol. I lost some weight and was feeling better, but my blood pressure was also a bit high. I was walking every day I wasn't working out at **Curves**, but I wasn't a whole lot healthier.

In June of 2016 I had elevated cholesterol and triglycerides, inflammation, elevated blood

The Healing Journey Continues

pressure, allergies, low energy and just didn't feel right. I had read **Skinny Chicks Don't Eat Salads** by Christine Avanti and found out about estrogen dominance that contributes to belly fat. I never knew how many foods produce phytoestrogens in our bodies until I was on the estrogen blocker and needed to avoid soy. Contrary to Christine's title, I do eat a lot of salads. They are not my favorite dish,
but it's an easy way to get a lot of veggies in my diet; especially if you chop them.
  Next, I read, **The High Blood Pressure Solution** by Richard D. Moore, M.D. PhD. and was all set to follow that doctor's plan. I checked with my own doctor and she did preliminary blood tests and okayed me to stop the diuretic and allergy medicine and see how the plan in the book worked for me.
  Before I got started on that plan, the next grace was the afternoon John and I saw Dr. Mark Hyman speak on our local PBS station during their pledge drive about his **Eat Fat,**

Get Thin book. His approach to food made sense to us. John said, "Look up that book and buy it!" So I did.

The Adventure Begins!

The first of July 2016, I began Dr. Hyman's twenty-one-day elimination diet and followed his eating guidelines, recipes, supplements and exercise. I walked for 30 minutes each morning before breakfast. I eliminated wheat/gluten, dairy, sugar-including natural sweeteners and high glycemic fruits, beans and legumes and other inflammatory foods. I also kept starchy vegetables for dinner as well as avoiding processed and prepared foods as he advised. Dr. Hyman talked a lot about leaky gut, so I took probiotic capsules and potato starch as a pre-biotic.

These 21 days got my sugar cravings under control, allergy symptoms that put me on allergy medicine all but disappeared and the inflammation that had put me on the diuretic subsided. My blood pressure normalized and by the end of fall, I'd lost 30 pounds from February, my highest weight. I've been within 10 pounds of my lowest weight for 3 ½ years, which seems to be my body's desirable weight.

Reading **Eat Fat, Get Thin** answered a lot of the questions I had about how my body works and where the low-fat "heart healthy" diet guidelines had come from such as the DASH diet. Dr. Hyman and Dr. Caroline Leaf both call our typical Modern American Diet the MAD diet; high in sugar, salt, processed foods, fast food; things that our body doesn't recognize as food, so it stores them in our

Musings Along Life's Journey
By Heidi Honey

fat cells. How many times have I looked at gummy fruit snacks and realized my body is craving the real

fruits, not the 'healthy' candy concoctions? He also talked about the connection with sugar and diseases such as Alzheimer's and arthritis and how scientists in labs were paid by sugar companies to prove sugar wasn't the main health problem, fats were.

After the twenty-one days ended, I followed the plan to reintroduce wheat and found the inflammation resumed, but ceased after a couple days off the wheat. The dairy reintroduction brought back my throat, nasal and sinus allergy symptoms as well as constipation. I felt so much better after just 21 days, I wanted to keep it that way!

Maintenance

I settled into eating the things that worked well with my body and avoiding or eliminating completely the ones that bothered me or exacerbated symptoms. I adapted Dr. Hyman's 'pegan' diet-a mixture of paleo and vegan- with lots of vegetables, healthy fats, good proteins, minimal sugars or high glycemic fruits. I also minimize beans and legumes because they're inflammatory to me. Dr. Hyman also stresses staying away from processed and fast foods, so we keep them to a minimum.

The Spirit led me to the book **Cooking For** found to be highly allergic to gluten and dairy when

The Adventure Begins!

Isaiah by Silvana Nardone. Her son Isaiah was he was fourteen, and having worked on Rachael Ray's cooking show, Silvana went out and got an array of food ingredients and worked in her kitchen until she'd perfected recipes that tasted as good as they looked and appealed to her family. I have several gluten-free cookbooks but have not found a gluten-free flour blend I like better than hers. I've also found **Ronzoni** has the best gluten-free pastas. My husband likes the gluten-free pizza I make with Silvana's recipe better than any other pizza we have had! My grandchildren love the banana pancakes and waffles I make from Silvana's recipes as well. Believe it or not, I've also used pureed beets in place of the banana and no one knew the difference!

These days, it is increasingly easier to find gluten-free and dairy free alternatives, and I've found I don't need to completely eliminate wheat and dairy anymore, but I try to be wise about my choices. I eat mozzarella or feta cheese and will have a piece of birthday cake and maybe a small scoop of ice cream occasionally. I still feel bad about attending my grandson's birthday party and refusing to eat a piece of cake while I was on the 21-day elimination; his mom had made a vegan cake with avocado frosting, but I was only three days away from the end of the elimination and had not eaten sugar or sweeteners to that point and didn't want to break my sugar fast.

I try not to bake chocolate chip cookies or brownies, even if they ARE gluten & dairy free, because there is still the sugar and calorie overload

Musings Along Life's Journey
By Heidi Honey

possibility, so they remain an occasional treat. Not to mention, it's also one of my Achilles heels my soul loves to overdose on!

Along with changing my eating habits and working more exercise into my routine, I've

stopped
concentrating on the pro- and pre-biotics now that my gut seems healthy. I still take a daily vitamin/ mineral supplement, vitamin D-3, Co-Q-10, and Omega 3 as well as psyllium husk fiber, but haven't had any prescriptions other than a couple years' trial of statin pills, and rarely take even one Tylenol.

I still have high cholesterol, but all my other levels are normal or below and my "good" cholesterol is rising. I have a new general practitioner who is more holistic, and she said it is my choice, so I've stopped taking the low dose statin. I find it interesting; Dr. Hyman recommends psyllium husk if you're gluten-free because you need the fiber that is scarce in the pegan diet, then my doctor told me it's the best thing for lowering LDL "bad" cholesterol.

Uniqueness

The biggest thing I found in all of this is each one of us is different. Our bodies are all human, but each one so unique and intricately put together by God that there's no 'one size fits all' plan that works for me *AND* for you. The best thing to do is eliminate things and reintroduce them slowly, keeping track of how your body responds. I've kept I mark down when I overdo or something's out of

The Adventure Begins!

a journal of my eating, medicines and supplements. whack, or I overeat things I don't regularly eat, or just don't feel good. I also note when I change any supplements or take any medicine. I did it daily in the beginning of the 21 days, writing down everything I ate as well as all supplements. When you must write everything down, it's a great way to curb what you eat. Currently, I note major changes in my supplements, eating, or things I note in my body when they occur so I can look back and see what worked and what didn't. I also food journal when I need to come back to center.

You can find support for any eating, diet or exercise plan, but quickly find another 'expert' that
says the opposite. Remember when eggs were the enemy? Now experts say one egg a day is good for your cholesterol. One big thing for health is keeping well-hydrated. The standard consensus is eight 8-ounce glasses a day with more if you are exerting yourself or are overweight. On the other hand, I read one report where the doctor said we only need about four cups of liquid a day and you can get most of that from the foods you eat. I remember my elderly grandmother drank nothing but hot tea. This is all very frustrating and confusing. The Bible uses food for metaphor often. It contains milk, bread, meat and honey. I've heard it explained as milk that even a baby understands, bread that is a bit harder to chew, meat that needs ruminating chewing, honey that's sweet, pleasurable, and

easy.

Musings Along Life's Journey
By Heidi Honey

Here's God's promise repeated to each generation of His chosen people from Moses.

If the LORD delights in us, then He will bring us into this land and give it to us, 'a land which flows with milk and honey.'
(Numbers 14:8)

Proverbs repeatedly uses honey as a metaphor.

My son eat honey because it is good, and the honeycomb which is sweet to your taste.
(Proverbs 24:13)

Have you found honey?
Eat only as much as you need,
lest you be filled with it and vomit.
(Proverbs 25:1
A satisfied soul loathes the honeycomb,
but to a hungry soul every bitter thing is sweet.
(Proverbs 27:7)

A conclusion I have come to is moderation in sweet things keeps you from getting sick.

The next verses show God's words are sweeter than honey, and His love is better than wine.

> *How sweet are Your words to my taste, Sweeter than honey to my mouth!*
> (Psalm 119:103)

The Adventure Begins!

> *Let him kiss me with the kisses of his mouth— For your love is better than wine.*
> (Song Of Solomon 1:2)

Exercise and Moderation

What does the Bible say about exercise? This is the only verse I've found that talks about bodily exercise:

> *For bodily exercise profits a little, but godliness is profitable for all things, having promise of the life that now is and of that which is to come.*
> (1 Timothy 4:8)

I exercise most days for about 30 minutes. Some days I take a walk, but since February 2020, it's been functional workouts in my living room with Pahla Bower most days. Her workouts can be found here:

www.pahlabfitness.com/www.pahlabsports.com She started as a preschool teacher, became a runner and is now certified both as a personal trainer and as a functional fitness trainer. She calls herself, "Pahla B, your best middle-aged fitness trainer". She aims her videos at women, but keeps it family friendly, knowing homes have children around. She's happy to hear younger women and men also enjoy her workouts!

Musings Along Life's Journey

By Heidi Honey

Most of her workouts are 23 minutes long, easy to fit in your schedule. She also has 10-minute videos you can stack to make your own workout, and stretching/cool-down videos if you didn't get enough in the 30 minutes. You'll find cardio, strength, balance, walking and running training. She stresses moderation, working on proper form to prevent injury, and balance and proprioception [perception or awareness of the position and movement of the body.(from the dictionary)] to prevent falls. Pahla
offers lots of choice, since she estimates she has recorded at least 1,000 workouts since she began doing exercise videos eight years

ago: as of March 2022!

She talks through the whole workout, giving you lots of tips, understanding and ways you can modify or moderate the workout to get what you need from it. Pahla also has short teaching videos to answer all your questions. There are myriad workout videos, but I believe the Lord led me to Miss Pahla B when I typed "Functional Fitness" in the search, and she has all I need to keep limber, strong, and balanced.

Yes, this bodily exercise profits me some by keeping me limber and in shape, giving me a good outlook due to the endorphins. But in reading articles over the past couple of years in Reader's Digest, I find getting 30-45 minutes of walking-inside, outside, treadmill or otherwise- or climbing four sets of stairs most days gives you enough exercise

The Adventure Begins!

for a normal person. Of course, none of this exercise is enough if I don't feed on the Word of God as well. My goal is to be as healthy as possible for as long as possible, to be fit for the plans the Lord has for me, but this does no good eternally if I'm lacking in Spiritual health. Milk feedings only go so far; these are ones we get second-hand as a mama bird feeds her young by regurgitating. This means Sunday morning service is not enough if you want your spirit to grow fat and healthy. If you go to my devotional chapter, you will see how I have worked at moderating that to a level that feeds me well too.

Sleep

Another aspect of health and well-being is sleep. I am reading **Seeing The Voice Of God** by Laura Harris Smith. She found herself in stage 3 adrenal burnout due to sleep deprivation. God intervened and healed her body, but it is an ongoing process. She talks about how much of our population is dangerously lacking sleep and if you are sleeping, many are sleeping too few hours to get a good sleep. Charity Virkler Kayembi also speaks and writes about sleep and dreams; God is really working to get us to a place where He can speak to us in our dreams.

God Knows

Our bodies are rejuvenated; healed while we sleep. When God created us, He knew we needed an average of 8 hours sleep to function properly. A

human is made of three parts: body, soul, and spirit. Just like God, our spirits never sleep, but our body and soul need to. This was a great revelation to me; I never consciously put all this together that my soul never sleeps.

> *He will not allow your foot to be moved;*
> *He who keeps you will not slumber.*
> *Behold, He who keeps Israel Shall*
> *neither slumber nor sleep.*
> (Psalm 121:3-4)

> *I sleep, but my heart is*
> *awake; It is the voice of*
> *my beloved!* (Song of
> Solomon 5:2a)

My sleep has been disrupted for many reasons. I am an intercessor. One teacher says they
are awakened at 2 a.m. to pray, another says intercessors will waken by the Holy Spirit in the night watches between 3 and 6 a.m. to pray. My husband is awake several times at night and when we are apart and compare, we seem to awaken at the same times frequently; 2,3,5/6a.m. are normal possibilities. When awakened, I have learned to pray for my husband and whomever else Holy Spirit brings to mind at these times. I often pray or sing in the Spirit [tongues/heavenly language] because my thoughts aren't usually clear enough to pray in English at these times.

The Adventure Begins!

Besides waking in the night seasons or night
watches, I stay up late some nights. I like reading and can get lost in a book, or watching a movie or video, or finishing a project that will only take "a few more minutes". I am so glad we have never had a T.V. in our bedroom!

Another one of my achilles heels is playing Mahjong games on the computer until my fingers hurt and my eyes grow bleary. As with all addictions, I just want to play a couple rounds, but keep going for hours some evenings… just one more round. It is also difficult if my day is either busy or sedentary. They both make it hard to prepare for sleep, being over tired or not tired enough. Mother used to say, "An hour of sleep before midnight is worth two hours after midnight." I have proved this true many a time! What does the Bible say?

It is vain for you to rise up early, to sit up late, to eat the bread of sorrows; for so He gives His beloved sleep.
(Psalm 127:2)

Remedies

I avoid caffeine and other things I know keep me from falling asleep. Sometimes I need to stop caffeine as early as noon! Some people like a "night cap" drink of wine or liquor before bed, but Laura Harris Smith shares that it will put you to sleep but will not keep you asleep. I have taken sleep aids, but they are all known to alter your sleep patterns and cause memory problems; stopping them makes it a struggle to get back to normal sleep on your own.

Musings Along Life's Journey
By Heidi Honey

I find magnesium supplements help, but I must take them right before bed instead of with supper; otherwise I get drowsy within an hour and then sleep eludes me later. I also use lavender essential oil with coconut oil for a carrier. Especially on the bottoms of your feet at bedtime, this and other calming oils can help you drift off sooner.

Some evenings I sip decaf tea, often **Sleepy Time** that helps calm my body down. My husband and I have made it a frequent evening routine, although not so much in the hotter weather. We take turns making the tea. He blesses me by putting a couple ice cubes in mine and delivering it to me, I bless him by putting a spoon full of honey in his and bringing it to him. It's a nice time to connect before bed at the end of a hectic day. There are several different bedtime teas available; I suggest you find one you like and drink it often.

As I settle to sleep, I do a few deep breaths, claim sweet sleep and sweet dreams from Father God, I thank the Holy Spirit for communing with my spirit as I sleep, and remind Father my body needs rest to recover. I trust He knows how much I need for that night. This is a good time to give thanks for Him guiding me through the day. I keep something to write on by my bed which allows me to release my mind from fretting about not remembering later. That is how much of this book has come to me; much of it on phone apps that have eaten up all my storage space!

The Adventure Begins!

To finish this chapter with balance, I share advice from the Apostle Paul.

> *[Glorify God in Body and Spirit] All things are lawful for me, but all things are not helpful. All things are lawful for me,*
> *but I will not be brought under the power of any.*
> *(1 Corinthians 6:12)*

And again:

> *[All to the Glory of God] All things are lawful for me, but not all things are helpful; all things are lawful for me, but not all things edify.*
> *(1 Corinthians 10:23)*

Conclusion:

I hope this chapter has encouraged you. My mother often said, "All things in moderation." I think this agrees with the Bible, although I don't find this exact proverb in the Bible. Dr. Kevin Zadai says our bodies are like an earth suit for our spirits, so we need to spend less time concentrating on them and more on the things of God. It is good to have a true estimation of yourself and follow the Apostle Paul's admonition:

> *For you were bought at a price; therefore glorify God in your body and in your spirit, which are God's.*
> (1 Corinthians 6:20)

Musings Along Life's Journey
By Heidi Honey

A little entertainment, relaxation, eating for pleasure or overtime work is okay, but if this is your goal, you'll find your life lacking. I look for grace to eat to live; not live to eat! I don't want to be a lover of sleep, but put sleep into proper perspective as well as food. As Paul did, let us choose to not be brought under the power of any earthly thing. Don't persist in things that are not edifying. Choose to follow our God addiction and drown in His love, grace and provision rather than the world's many addictions that never quite satisfy. In these days we live in, walking in faith and victory is the key to
an overcoming life. We cannot do it without a close relationship with Father God, Lord Jesus, and Holy Spirit. I encourage you to seek the Lord for the daily grace He provides.

His compassion and mercy are new every morning as Lamentations chapter three says:

Through the LORD's mercies we are not consumed, because His compassions fail not. They are new every morning; great is Your faithfulness.
                  (Lamentations 3:22-23)

He Has Gone Before Me

Praise God, challenges strengthen our faith! His mercy and grace truly are sufficient, as we learn to live by faith and realize He has gone before us. Here I share several instances from my experiences from
spring of 2018.

Car In Culvert

On May 17 I had rushed my plant cuttings to the Treadwell's barn to add to the Garden Club plant sale that was being set up that Friday for the Saturday sale. Pulling on the grass next to another car, I had a little chat with Sara Treadwell while I unloaded my pots. I'd had a quick thought that I should have backed in when I parked, but I'd ignored it.

When I was done, I got back in the car to rush back to the house because we were taking our son Chris to the city to have a back treatment and my husband John was anxious to leave. My Mom often quoted an old Pennsylvania Dutch proverb: "The hurrier I go, the behinder I get." This was one of those times that maxim was true!

As I started backing out, I could not quite see where I was in relation to the culvert. Well, I managed to get my car hung up with the right front wheel spinning over the abyss of that culvert. I got

Musings Along Life's Journey
By Heidi Honey

out and saw how close I came to falling in; I'm sure an angel had intervened!

God's grace and provision continued: a neighbor passing by stopped with his truck, eager to help, but had nothing in his truck to hook up to my car. I called John and calmly told him I needed help. The next grace came when John showed up with our son, Chris, who said: "Good thing I decided to come early!" John followed with: "I'm glad our son Alex gave me this tow strap that's been in the back seat of my truck!"

The neighbor who had stopped helped guide John's truck into place, then Chris got the tow strap attached and got in the car to drive while John pulled. The neighbor and Sara helped stabilize the car as it came back onto solid ground. I looked on; my heart was singing! No damage to the car and we got Chris to his appointment in good time. Sara assured me I was not the first to have ended up in the culvert and was able to put a caution sign by the culvert before the sale. I've vowed never again to think about damaging grass; I will back up and pull out frontward when parking from now on—ALWAYS! Oh, the plant sale went very well the next day, even in the rain.

Blown Tire

A couple weeks after the culvert challenge, I was driving back from Lowville, heard a noise toward the back of the car, then the low tire light came on.

He Has Gone Before Me

I drove just a bit more and realized I must have a flat tire. Not wanting to pull to the side of the main road, I drove slowly onto the next side road.

Again, I knew who was in charge and was calm. I had helped John take off the snow tires and put on the regular ones less than a month before, so I knew I couldn't change the tire by myself. The first driveway I pulled into, no one was at home. I limped the car to the second house and an older man answered the door. I told him I had a flat tire and couldn't change it myself but could help.

He yelled back to his wife what was going on, then came out through the garage as I was digging out the tire changing stuff and the spare tire. Good news: I had a full-sized spare in my trunk!

The "good Samaritan" had a Vietnam Veteran hat on, so I had a topic of conversation to start with. He brought out his big jack, but we had to use the car's jack to get it under the frame due to the flat tire.

We efficiently worked together to get the tire changed. I packed up my trunk and thanked him for being there in my time of need. Praise God, it was still light out at almost 8 p.m., that the man was home and willing and able to help and had the tools we needed.

I took off and drove a bit slower the last half hour home to Henderson, while I talked to John on the car phone. He was concerned the tire rim was

Musings Along Life's Journey
By Heidi Honey

ruined, an extra expense along with having to buy two new tires to balance the car. He hashed and re-hashed all the worst-case scenarios and I just rested in the peace of God while I commiserated with him.

After making it home safely, I looked on-line for new rim and tire and was surprised at the cost. Volkswagen parts tend to be more expensive

than parts for other cars we've owned, but again I rejoiced in having the full-sized spare tire!

Next morning, John came from Lowville. He found the rim was not damaged because the side of the tire blew out and cushioned it; praise God! We went into Sam's Club to look at tires. They had a good discount for buying four tires at once, so John decided to buy all four. They were able to change my tires while we drove John's truck over to Lowe's to get things he needed for the project in Lowville. He had planned to get new tires for the car the next spring, but the Lord had other plans! Thank You, Father God, for providing the finances to re-tire the car.

Road Trip?

John was planning a Father/Son Alaskan fishing trip with our son Harold, his father-in-law and brother-in-law, our daughter's husband and his father. My two sisters and a niece's family live in Virginia, so John had suggested I could plan a trip to visit while he was in Alaska.

Musings Along Life's Journey
By Heidi Honey

I planned to travel four of the six days

he'd be on his trip. The plan was: my daughter-in-law and her two daughters would go with me, so I had company driving. After the two previous adventures with my car, I was bolstered in my faith and trusting the Lord to keep me. I knew angels had ministered and guided my car, knew Father God has it all under control and was faithful to provide all we needed, that Jesus inside me is mighty, and Holy Spirit guides me.

Imagine my surprise when John told me he was not comfortable with me traveling while he was gone. He talked about getting Triple A insurance coverage
for me with the car troubles I'd had. He made know he wasn't opposed to me visiting my family, but not while he was too far away to help if I needed. He made a comment that he can't go on "blind faith".

Well, the Lord's been working on my heart, so I kept calm and let go of my plans after texting my sisters and daughter-in-law. It worked out well that I didn't leave the "homestead" the end of June into July. The garden ended up needing a lot of watering and I had work at the motel while John was gone.

By the way, John got stuck in the airport in the lower 48 overnight on his way to Alaska due to weather delays and connection problems. He got to the Alaska fishing a day late, but our son, Harold, had waited for him. They went out to fish that afternoon and limited out quickly. God was faithful to them!

He Has Gone Before Me

I am finding life going much easier as I learn to trust and obey the Lord. Through our growing relationship, I'm learning more about my husband as my authority-beneath Jesus-covering me. I'm also learning to let go and not take things personally, which has been a struggle all my life. Making this choice and walking in it, I've sensed a burden lifted from my shoulders and it's eased my mind. I want to walk by faith more each day, going deeper into my relationship with Emmanuel, God with us.

Yes, Before Me!

Andrew and John Eastmond (you can find them at www.andreweastmond.com) came to minister at our church September 20, 2019. After wonderful ministry in song and John's wonderful guitar prowess, Andrew started a line for those who wanted prayer and prophecy. Since I never want to miss a chance to hear God, I went forward. Andrew's word for me is where this chapter came from. I'd like to share a bit of what he said by the Spirit.

"You're the God of all comfort, in the difficult places, rough places, and potholes and bumps in the road, I promise you things are gonna smooth out. It's like when we've been on a really rough road and suddenly come onto a whole new piece of blacktop. Even our car goes 'aah'.

That's how your life's been going; you've been negotiating potholes and bumps. It's time for new blacktop; new ground in Jesus' name. You're gonna know that God has gone before you; you'll say, "God's

Musings Along Life's Journey
By Heidi Honey

been here before me. This couldn't be going this well if He didn't go before me." So you're going to have the testimony. "Wow! He actually went down the road ahead of me; behind me; No, no, no! He was ten miles down the road ahead of me too, smoothing it out."

This word resonated with me. My many trips between Lowville and Henderson have been bumpy with humps from the weather and potholes. In the middle of the trip, there are several stretches of newly paved road. Yes, I and my car say "Aah". Also, Kevin Zadai shared Psalm139 in the Passion translation, pointing out the fact that God goes before us clearing out the way and leading us, goes behind us to keep us from the pain of the past, and has His hand of blessing on our heads. How good is our God that He would orchestrate the happenings in my life to align with what His prophet said to me!

Many are saying that 2020 is the year of perfect vision. One man recently said 2015 is perfect vision, 2020 is about hindsight which gives us answers. I believe this year of chaos in government, conflicting reports about this viral (or is it bacterial?) pandemic and our being sequestered in our homes give lots of time for us to seek the Lord and let the Spirit illuminate things. I do not believe the upsets, chaos and such will let up before the end of this world comes; rather Jesus told us they will increase, so this is relevant no matter when you are reading it. It's an opportunity to take stock of what's gone before to start understanding what is next to come.

He Has Gone Before Me

I know this is true in my own life and hope it is in yours also. I pray that you will not be one of the many whose heart grows cold as the world grows dark like the Apostle Paul said.

Oh, I've noticed several times in the Scriptures God tells us not to be in awe of what the enemy is doing; but to look to Him and stand in awe of what He is doing!

Becoming as a Child

I have been contemplating what it means to become as a little child. What did Jesus mean when He said that?

> Then Jesus called a little child to Him, set him in the midst of them, and said, "Assuredly, I say to you, unless you are converted and become as little children, you will by no means enter the kingdom of heaven." Therefore whoever humbles himself as this little child is the greatest in the kingdom of heaven.
> (Matthew 18:2-4)

Now I'd like to talk about becoming as a child. What does this really mean? Jesus doesn't say to become childish, but to become like a child. A child is trusting, believes that their Daddy has what they need and what's best, and will give them what they ask for. I've heard and can see: the biggest sin in the church today is unbelief. If we pray and don't believe God is willing and able to answer those prayers, we are in unbelief. We serve a prayer hearing, prayer answering God. Let's take Him at His word.

Musings Along Life's Journey
By Heidi Honey

I want to share this quote from K.P. Yohannan's book **Never Give Up,** *The Story of a Broken Man Impacting a Generation.*

"All that is needed to be said [in defending God's existence] is God is the Creator and we are His creation, and we as believers don't ask God to prove Himself to us. We are like little kids. We don't ask our mother and father if they are our parents-we are their children, and they are our parents, and that's it-period!" page 100

Another quality of children is humility. In our culture, we do not see humility in a good light. It doesn't mean weakness; it means knowing your true worth and walking in that true estimation of your position relative to Jesus and Father God. According to the Bible, Jesus humbled Himself to come from heaven to earth, ultimately to die a criminal's death on a cross. It is not control, but a loving Father knowing your needs and wanting to fill them the right way. Let me tell you a couple stories about these things in my life.

The Lost Lamb

Note: I home-schooled my youngest son, Alexander, from third-sixth grade. One spring day when he was about ten, he was helping our friend, Mel Zehr, clean their family campgrounds. Alex told me when he was young that Mel was a 'good Grandpa' and they had a close relationship; especially while he was home-schooling.

Becoming as a Child

During the cleaning, he found a little toy lamb, lost and forlorn, under a trailer. His soft heart could not leave it lying there in the dirt, so he brought it home to see what I could do with it.

The poor toy was dirty, and its head was almost separated from its body. Because my son saw it as something worth bringing home, I set to work mending and cleaning. After putting the stuffing back in and stitching the neck back onto the body, I washed it and was amazed to see how clean the little lamb turned out. I found a royal-looking purple ribbon and tied it in a bow around the mended neck.

Isn't this a true picture of the lost lamb Jesus went after when He left the ninety-nine behind? He took the time to find the lamb, rescue and comfort it; all the time rejoicing that the lamb was returned to the fold. In the same way I cleaned and cared for the toy lamb, rejoicing to see how clean it became, Jesus tends to our wounds, cleans us whiter than snow by His blood, and then adopts us into the royal
family of Father God.

This little toy lamb has been sitting on a shelf in my bedroom for many years, reminding me of the Lord's goodness. It also reminds me of a young boy's faith in the Lord as he was learning to trust Him.

Musings Along Life's Journey
By Heidi Honey

A Parable of the Lost Lamb

"The Son of Man has come to give life to anyone who is lost. Think of it this way: If a man owns a hundred sheep and one lamb
wanders away and is lost, won't he leave the ninety-nine grazing on the hillside and go out

and thoroughly search for the one lost lamb? And if he finds his lost lamb, he rejoices over it, more than over the ninety-nine who are safe. Now you should understand that it is never the desire of your heavenly Father that a single one of these humble believers should be lost."
            (Matthew 18:11-14)

One January evening as the membership

roll was being called at our church's annual meeting, I began thinking about my children who have walked away from church, as well as other young people they grew up with who have done the same. The Lord began illuminating these Scriptures for me and applying them to my life.

The shepherd left 99 of his sheep to go after the one sheep that strayed away. Would you leave behind 99% of your assets to save 1%? I'm sure your financial advisor wouldn't recommend it!

Becoming as a Child

As with this stray one, many people have strayed away from our churches, our families, the values they were taught when young. They have fallen into the crevices left by the world and all it contains;
tasting of what their elders forbid them when they were young, under house rules.

As a shepherd seeks for his stray lamb, so our Lord seeks for the lost, particularly our wayward children. He will seek until He finds them, whatever deep, dark crevasse of the enemy they have fallen into. Our children will return to the Lord just as the Good Shepherd returned the lost one to the fold. He will carry them gently; wash their wounds and
pour in the oil and wine that restore their souls. By faith, those who have wandered away

will surely be brought back into the fold. Then there will be great rejoicing!

Addictions

Recently in our Life Group (small group that gathers once a week), our leaders, Tom and Peggy Giles, said their adult children were talking about all the people cutting themselves, the suicides and drug addictions in their contemporaries. I said something and Peggy told me to write down: "We haven't invested in the little ones, and the families are not being families, so they have no love resource to draw from, so they have no identity." In other words, the parents haven't been taught their worth in God, they can't share love they've never learned, so the children have not learned how to love themselves.

Musings Along Life's Journey
By Heidi Honey

I've learned from Dan Mohler that the people who hurt you were dry cups and had nothing to give you. If you hold it against them, you become just as dry, hurtful and lacking in love as they were to you. Nobody owes me anything; in the Bible, the Apostle Paul says we should owe no one anything but love.

Perry Stone on his, **Keys To Praying For Prodigal Children** CD, says that the same oxytocin/ pleasure centers in our brain and body are activated by all addictive behaviors. I learned in my Care Net training that it only takes 37 seconds of close contact to form a bond. The hormones responsible for this are the same ones that bond a mother to her baby as she nurses it. That's a strong connection!

God created us to be addicted to His Word, His presence, His love. When we fill this part of us with other things, like food, entertainment, shopping, drugs, pornography, violence... you get the picture: it's difficult to wean ourselves from it. Oxytocin is a powerful hormone.

Although some imbalances need to be addressed by medications for a time to balance things and there's no shame in seeking medical help, years of therapy can be avoided by Holy Spirit power coming in and removing desires, burning away the chaff, healing the body, mind and soul. In other words, if you know who you are in Christ, you are freed from the lies you grew up with.

Becoming as a Child

Dr. Caroline Leaf says it takes twenty-one days to replace a bad habit with a good one, then usually two more twenty-one-day cycles, or just over two months, to change your habits long-term. I can testify that a few years ago when I followed Dr. Leaf's advice, as little as seven minutes a day in a quiet place speaking the truths of God over myself for twenty-one days changed my thought process. This has brought me to a new level of being healed.

If we don't despair over our children or ourselves, triumph will come. I find myself declaring promises from the Word of God. As for me and my house, we shall serve the Lord. [Joshua 24:15]...*me and my whole household shall be saved.* [Acts 16:31], *that the eyes of their understanding be open...*

[Ephesians 1:18], also: my children shall be taught of the Lord; great will be their peace [Isaiah 54:13]. I also call to the Lord of the Harvest to send out more workers, and my loved ones are workers for the harvest [Luke 10:2].

As we keep standing in the gap, interceding for our children, the Lord will draw them back in. We need to be walking in love toward them; not rehearsing and despairing in the things we see going on in their lives. As we speak life and God's purposes for them, without doubting, God's will for them to be saved shall be accomplished. I have come to realize if my spirit never sleeps, theirs do not either. Ask the Holy Spirit to woo their spirits to Jesus as they sleep.

Musings Along Life's Journey
By Heidi Honey

Trust in the LORD, and do good, dwell in the land, and feed on His faithfulness. Delight yourself also in the LORD, and He shall give you the desires of your heart. Commit your way to the LORD, trust also in Him, And He shall bring it to pass. He shall bring forth your righteousness as the light, and your justice as the noonday.
(Psalm 37:3-6)

Trust, Dwell, Feed, Delight, Commit; trust also in Him—sounds like words that lead to child-like faithfulness when heeded.

What about you? Have you humbled yourself as a trusting child and let Jesus come into your life? Do you know what it's like to have your dirty sins washed clean? Are you a part of the Royal Family with Jesus as King; welcomed into the fold to rest on Father God's lap? Do you trust the One who holds the stars in place to hold the things you release to Him?

Jewish Thoughts

My father's mother was Jewish. As I have matured, interest in Jewish things and Israel has increased. I've thought a lot about a phrase Sid Roth uses: 'One New Man' which was formed when Jesus made the New Covenant in His blood which reconciled Jew and Gentile [anyone who's not Jewish] to each other and to God. What a wonder! In my own bloodline, Jew and Gentile joined as one when my grandparents wed, so in the natural I'm 'One New Man', as well as in the Spiritual. I count myself doubly blessed.

My Heritage

When dating, Dad did not tell Mom his mother was Jewish because he was afraid she would not marry him if she knew. My mother's family was not like that, but Dad had lived through a lot of trouble with his staunch, bigoted German father and Austrian Jewish mother. My grandmother, Trudi, was a gem. I remember she had a beautiful Menorah that her cousin Erica got her in Israel. We helped her light the candles during Hanukkah when we visited. She also had a good set of china in the cupboard over the refrigerator that only came out for Passover. It was a treat to have buttered Matzah in her kitchen.

If she ate Easter dinner with us during Passover, she could eat the Easter eggs, but not a lot of the rest of the meal. My grandfather tolerated her "religious" stuff. If you ever watched the T.V.

Musings Along Life's Journey
By Heidi Honey

show, "**All In The Family**," it was very similar to my grandparent's life in their little trailer.

When I started asking her about her journey to America and her life in Austria, which she had emigrated from when she was ten –in 1914– she was a bit surprised. She thought none of us was interested in her heritage or learning German. I wrote an essay for my social studies teacher in eleventh grade called, "The Ship Veered Toward the Mine." I told how my grandmother left Vienna with her mother in 1914 and when they reached their ship, the English Channel was already beset with bombs. Before so many Holocaust and World War II stories came out, this was my early connection to the story of my own family's Jewish wanderings.

As I'm finding out more about the Jewish culture and the history of Israel as a nation and as a people, I've noticed some things that blessed me. My four siblings and myself were my grandmother Trudi's only grandchildren; my father was an only child. My eldest sister, Gretchen, was born-again in 1972; so was Sid Roth. It was also the year eleven Israeli athletes were murdered at the Munich Olympics. My brother Karl was born in 1956, the year of the "Suez Campaign." My brother Friedrich (Fritz) was born in 1958, when this event occurred in Israel: The Knesset passes the first Basic Law to established and define the electoral system. I was born May 14, 1963, the fifteenth anniversary of Israel being declared a Nation, which fulfilled the prophecy that a Nation would miraculously be born

Jewish Thoughts

in a day. My sister, Trina, was born in 1967, the year of Israel's Six Day war which reunited the Old and New sections of Jerusalem under Jewish control for the first time in contemporary history.
Let's look into a few more things on this Jewish topic.

Columbus in 1492

Maybe you remember the little ditty we sang in elementary school: 'Columbus sailed the ocean blue in fourteen hundred ninety-two'. We learned he went to King Ferdinand and Queen Isabella of Spain to ask for ships to sail to the

New World. Did you know Christopher Columbus was Jewish? He must have been "incognito" [as my Dad was before marriage]. In 1492 Spain was persecuting the Jewish people who had lived there for generations. They were given the choice of converting to Catholicism, being killed, or leaving the country. Well, you know the story: Columbus got the ships and sailed to the New World.

I've recently learned that many of the family names in Mexico have Jewish roots. Columbus' journey made way for many of the persecuted Jewish Spaniards to leave Spain. A lot of Jewish people also relocated to Argentina. I know this because my Grandma Trudy's cousin Otto Mestler, married a Jewish woman from Argentina.

Musings Along Life's Journey
By Heidi Honey

What Did Rabbis Know?

The Jewish leaders in Jesus' time knew the books of the Law and the Prophets from childhood. They knew the prophecies that described the promised Messiah but did not recognize Jesus was the fulfillment of those ancient prophecies. Can you relate? In the Bible, we still have promise after promise from God for our life, our families, our times and seasons. Do we recognize and claim them often?

The Bible says the Bereans searched the Scriptures and understood the times and seasons they were living in. This is a good example to follow. Let's look at some things that they knew that will shed some light on familiar Scriptures. I have owned the **Complete Jewish Bible** and now own the **One New Man Bible** and have learned some interesting cultural things about events so familiar from the Bible. They have helped me make more sense and find more meaning in familiar passages.

Signs of Messiah

One of the things the Messiah was to do was heal a man born blind. Jesus did this several times! In John 9:6 and Mark 8:23

Jesus used His spit to heal the blind men. Jewish tradition believed the spittle of the eldest son contained healing ability. Two more signs of Messiah the religious people missed were: raising a person from the dead and healing one deaf from birth. This is why they gave

Jewish Thoughts

Jesus such a hard time when He performed these miracles; it blew their theology because He didn't look like they expected the Messiah to look!

What about the woman with the issue of blood? [Matthew 9:20, Mark 5:25-26, Luke 8:43-44] Most translations say she touched the hem of His robe or garment. Jesus followed Jewish tradition, wearing a 'Tallit', prayer shawl. The prayer shawl has longer tassels on the outer edges called 'Tzit Tzit' which are believed to have healing properties. Reading the Scripture in this light, the woman knew this and reached out to touch the closest of His Tzit Tzit. It would have been awkward to touch the hem of His robe; she most likely would have ended up on the ground behind him if she reached that low. Mark 5:30 says Jesus knew that "virtue" or power had gone out of Him. Oh, that we would be so filled and conscious of Holy Spirit power within that we would notice when it was drawn out of us!

In **The Glory Has Come**, *Encountering The Wonder of Christmas* [An Advent Devotional] compiled by Larry Sparks, I read about Simeon and Anna, who were in the Temple when Jesus' parents brought Him in to be dedicated. I find looking up what names mean in the Bible enhances my understanding of what I'm reading, so here I go.

And behold, there was a man in Jerusalem whose name was Simeon, and this man was just and devout, waiting for the Consolation of Israel, and the Holy Spirit was upon him. And it had been revealed to him by the Holy

Musings Along Life's Journey
By Heidi Honey

Spirit that he would not see death before he had seen the Lord's Christ. So he came by the Spirit into the temple. And when the parents brought in the Child Jesus, to do for Him according to the custom of the law...
(Luke 2:25-27)

In Hebrew, Simeon means: Obedient; listening; little hyena (https://meaning-of-names.com/ hebrewnames/simeon.asp).

Now there was one, Anna, a prophetess, the daughter of Phanuel, of the tribe of Asher. She was of a great age, and had

lived with a husband seven years from her virginity; and this woman was a widow of about eighty-four years, who did not depart from the temple, but served God with fastings and prayers night and day. And coming in that instant she gave thanks to the Lord, and spoke of Him to all those who looked for redemption in Jerusalem.
(Luke 2:36-38)

In Hebrew, Anna means: Favour or grace. Prayer. God has favoured me. Variant of Hannah, https:// meaning-of-names.com/hebrew-names/anna.asp [accessed May 2, 2020].

What I recently heard: Simeon stands for Old Testament Law, Anna stands for New Testament grace.

Jewish Thoughts

We try to make Biblical things fit into our chronological Gregorian calendar while the Jewish calendar is lunar, following the moon cycles. Our calendars make many Biblical matters confusing.

I recently learned the book of Revelation is not written chronologically. When you try to read it figuring out what the sequence of events is and what has occurred and what's to come, it is confusing. John had the visions in

segments. For one example: at about the time the vision was written down, people
could not buy or sell in the Agora market without the mark of the beast on their hand or forehead. I think it also happened in Russia during the communist era. Just when you think, "This is it!" you find this apparent fulfillment of prophecy has already been fulfilled, is being fulfilled and will be fulfilled again. That is part of what Jesus means when He says I am the one who was, and who is, and who is to come. [Revelation 1:4 & 8, 4:8, 11:17] Then James says with Father God there is no variation, no shadow; God's light is constant and never changes.

> *Every good gift and every perfect gift is from above, and comes down from the Father of lights, with whom there is no variation or shadow of turning.*
> (James 1:17)

Another important thing I've learned from Rabbi Jim Appel's Passover book is the Jews were allowed to celebrate the Passover Seder on either of two days due to how far flung the Jewish people were (and are) amongst the nations. This made it so Jesus

Musings Along Life's Journey

By Heidi Honey

could celebrate the 'last supper' with His

disciples on the first day and be our Passover Lamb on the second day. Also, did you ever wonder how Jesus could be in the grave three days if He died Friday afternoon and was raised from the dead Sunday morning? Jesus said He would be in the grave three days and three nights as Jonah was in the belly of the whale.

Going back to the two days for Passover. If Jesus died Friday and rose Sunday, that's three days, but only two nights. In the Appointed Times Series **FIRSTFRUITS** written by Rabbi Jim Appel he discusses the timing of Jesus' death and resurrection.

"The way we understand the timing, to make it correct—three days and three nights- it was on Wednesday evening that He had the Last Seder (also called the Last Supper)." page 86

Holy Spirit

On that note, let's talk a bit about The Holy Spirit, the third person of the Trinity. Although He is the neglected third person of the Holy Trinity by many today, the people in the Old Testament knew about Him; how He came upon certain people at certain times. The Jewish leaders also knew the

Jewish Thoughts

High Priest appointed to go into the Holy of Holies once a year was given a heavenly language only the priest, God, or an angel could understand and the devil and demons could not. Today, in fulfillment of Joel's prophecy, we are still reaping the benefits of Holy Spirit being poured out on all flesh. This year we celebrate Pentecost on May 23, 2021. The day of Pentecost is also known as First Fruits, the celebration Jews observe 50 days after Passover. For us in the church, it's 50 days after Christ's resurrection day.

Pentecost

Here is the account in Acts.

When the Day of Pentecost had fully come, they were all with one accord in one place. And suddenly there came a sound from heaven, as of a rushing mighty wind, and it filled the whole house where they were sitting. Then there appeared to them divided tongues, as of fire, and one sat upon each of them. And they were all filled with the Holy Spirit and began to speak with other tongues, as the Spirit gave them utterance.
(Acts 2:1-4)

This was the First Fruits of Joel's prophecy being fulfilled on the day of First Fruits.

And I will pray the Father, and He will give you another Helper, that He may abide with you forever—the Spirit of truth, whom the world cannot receive, because it neither sees

Musings Along Life's Journey

By Heidi Honey

Him nor knows Him; but you know Him, for He dwells with you and will be in you.
(John 14:16-17)

Jesus imparted a portion of Holy Spirit which came from Him, to the seventy disciples He sent out to the villages. When He visited the gathered disciples after his resurrection, Jesus breathed on them and told them to receive the Holy Spirit. On Pentecost, after waiting in the Upper Room, Holy Spirit came upon them as a rushing wind and tongues of flame, immersing them. This time they didn't have just a portion, but they were saturated in Holy Spirit! This is what gave them the ability to speak in other tongues, speaking to Jews gathered from all the nations able to hear the Gospel in their own language.

Notice Jesus says the Holy Spirit will abide with us forever. How did people get the idea Holy Spirit was only for the first Apostle's benefit? Do we need less comfort, teaching and leading now than the first Believers did? Do you need Holy power to thrive in these days? Another lie the devil has propagated with special help from religious leaders, is the gifts of the Spirit, including prophecy and healings, stopped after the Apostolic age. How sad! Most -if not all- the books in the New Testament talk about the Holy Spirit, signs, wonders, miracles, healings and deliverance.

Jewish Thoughts

If you study the Old Testament, you see everything in the New Testament confirms the Old; though you may have to piece Scriptures together in order to understand. We can still miss a lot of these topics, even if we have read the Bible through from cover to cover.

Every book in our Bible talks about the Love of God and His plan of redemption. It was only a year ago when I started reading the book of Revelation in a Red-Letter edition and realized it is Jesus speaking to John and not an angel. I was probably told this before but didn't remember. This realization puts a whole new light on these revelations given to John, along with the realization the book is not written chronologically!

Let us look at Peter's sermon in Acts Chapter 2:16-18:

But this is what was spoken by the prophet Joel: 'And it shall come to pass in

the last days, says God, That I will pour out of My Spirit on all flesh; Your sons and your daughters shall prophesy, Your young men shall see visions,
Your old men shall dream dreams. And on My menservants and on My maidservants I will pour out My Spirit in those days; And they shall prophesy.'

Are you a son or daughter? Are you a manservant? A maidservant? You may be a young man or an old man. What does this passage say you shall do? God's

Musings Along Life's Journey

By Heidi Honey

Spirit is poured out on all flesh. Sons and daughters shall prophesy, young men shall see visions, old men shall dream dreams. If that was not clear enough, the menservants and maidservants shall prophesy as well.

My Supernatural Experience

When I began attending evening service at Rhema Mennonite Fellowship in Lowville, NY the month of December 1986, Pastor Penn Clark was teaching on the gifts of Holy Spirit. Many churches teach people against the Holy Spirit, but I knew little about it. As people in the Bible say, "We have not so much as heard that there is a Holy Spirit." My sister Gretchen sent me a pamphlet from Women's Aglow on the Holy Spirit and how to receive Him.

As I sat nursing my seven-month-old son, reading the pamphlet, I asked the Holy Spirit to come in, found what sounded like baby talk forming in my head, and chose to speak it out since I had a baby in my lap! I stood up, still speaking in unknown syllables when I realized I'd rolled my r's, which I spent two years in Spanish class not being able to do. I told the devil he couldn't lie to me anymore; I knew for sure God is real because I know I couldn't do that myself. I started leaping and twirling with joy unspeakable!

Turns out you just ask Holy Spirit to come into your heart just like you did with Jesus to make Him your Savior. My baby loved to have me speak in tongues when he was in his crib or I was carrying him around.

People often tell me they don't hear God, they accepted Holy Spirit but can't speak in tongues,

Musings Along Life's Journey
By Heidi Honey

they've spoken in tongues but don't think they're doing it right, or they're just wasting breath. Some want to know how they can be sure it's not a tongue of the devil!

> *If a son asks for bread from any father among you, will he give him a stone? Or if he asks for a fish, will he give him a serpent instead of a fish? Or if he asks for an egg, will he offer him a scorpion? If you then, being evil, know how to give good gifts to your children, how much more will your heavenly Father give the Holy Spirit to those who ask Him!"*
> (Luke 11:11-13)

I have met people who don't mind talking about the Holy Spirit but have no personal experience with Him. Yes, Holy Spirit is part of salvation when you ask Jesus in, but the immersion is another thing. It's like my salvation experience. I didn't notice anything different, but had to believe I asked Jesus in and He came in. Three years later, I asked Holy Spirit in, and He came in, evidenced with speaking in tongues of men and angels.

We lack Spiritual power when we deny the Holy Spirit in-filling, the power within us. Using Holy Spirit language is yielding to the Spirit and letting Him use your tongue. You are still in control and can start and stop as an act of your will, but you can also flow in the Spirit, trusting Him to work through you. I've heard it compared to digging a hole with a shovel when there's a backhoe sitting beside you,

My Supernatural Experience

warmed up and ready to go. Maybe a pencil and paper when there's a top-of-the line computer beside you? I find the more I use the gift of tongues, the more the holy language grows and flows. If you've only tried it once, you don't know what you are missing!

> *Likewise, the Spirit also helps in our weaknesses; for we do not know what we should pray for as we ought, but the Spirit Himself makes intercession for us with groanings which cannot be uttered.*
> (Romans 8:26)

I quickly run out of things to say when I

pray, or I have so many things to pray for that I don't know where to start. This is when I am thankful I can pray in tongues and Holy Spirit can use my tongue to pray perfect prayers. I may be praying for someone around the globe from me, my next-door neighbor, or my children's grandchildren. From what I've read in the Bible, I am not only praying perfect prayers, but also giving thanks well. I encourage you to press into the Lord and allow Holy Spirit access to your faculties.

Pastor Penn shared the story of a man who was at an altar praying in tongues. The woman beside him turned to him and said, "How do you know my dialect of Mandarin Chinese?" He said, "I don't, but the Holy Spirit does!" Another story I heard was a Jewish woman who came to know Messiah. She asked God for a sign that she was doing the right thing being baptized. As she approached the baptismal, a woman speaking in tongues spoke perfect Hebrew,

Musings Along Life's Journey
By Heidi Honey

telling her Jesus is Messiah and baptism is Mikvah. The woman got her answer from God through the Holy Spirit by the obedience of that woman! I know when I sing and pray in the Holy Spirit, it's easier to pray in English and easier to have a word to give to someone else. It opens connection from my end to the God of the universe who is always there.

In my life, Holy Spirit has been the strong comforter Jesus said He would send us. His comfort allows me to comfort others in their time of need the way I have been comforted. Speaking of sending the Holy Spirit down. Did you know the Father sent the Holy Spirit when Jesus ascended to heaven? I don't know what I would do without Him leading and guiding, teaching and bringing things to mind. He makes me sound wise, intelligent, and creative despite or in spite of my training and education. He provides me with a song in my head. Having gone through short periods of not having that song in my head woke me up, bringing me back to the Word and my relationship with Him! The joy deep in my soul that bubbles out to encourage others also comes from the Spirit dwelling within me.

I recommend you find a booklet called, "**Why Tongues**," by Kenneth E. Hagin for a succinct explanation of this subject. He includes the verses in the Bible that talk about all of this.

Saved From The Fire?

'I will show wonders in heaven above and signs in the earth beneath: Blood and fire and vapor of smoke. The sun shall be turned into darkness, and the moon into blood, before the coming of the great and awesome day of the LORD. And it shall come to pass that whoever calls on the name of the LORD
Shall be saved.'

(Acts 2:19-21)

Have you observed God's wonders shown in the heavens (firmament) and on the earth? Things in the sky that you wonder about. All these signs that come before the day of the LORD have not come to pass yet, but they are soon to be. We long for the day Jesus returns, but it is not just glorious. It will also be great and awesome; terrible and terrifying. Are you ready? God says whoever calls on the name of the LORD shall be saved. There is no other name under heaven or on earth by which a man, woman or child may be saved; none but Jesus.

Are you assured of your destiny? If tonight is your last breath here on earth, do you know where you will spend eternity?

So what does salvation in Jesus' name mean? Is it just fire insurance to keep you out of hell when you die? Or does it mean something else?

Some people, especially in the U.S., tell people, "If you accept Jesus as your personal savior, your

Musings Along Life's Journey
By Heidi Honey

life will be perfect; easy! All your troubles will disappear." We do a disservice to people with this
line of talk. When I visited Ukrainian Believers, they stress to prospective converts that it will not be easy accepting Jesus. They need to be ready to face persecution, the possible loss of family and friends, or even their life with this choice. This was especially important during communism; the walls literally had ears, and you never knew if you could trust even a relative or best friend—let alone a new convert-even out in the country!

My Journey

I grew up being taken to church for Sunday School; dropped off by my father or walking to church with my elder siblings. Mom didn't go to church when we were young; it was her time with Dad and the Sunday newspaper. I remember getting a **Good News Bible** when I was in fourth grade, learning John 3:16 and memorizing the Ten Commandments to get a ribbon made of cardboard, markers and ribbon. The first time I brought my Bible to Sunday school, I remember getting glue and glitter on it during our craft time; great way to christen a new Bible! I also remember my two brothers had to wear black pants, a white button-down shirt, and skinny black tie to go to Sunday school. One day I asked Dad why my brother Karl wasn't in the car with us.

He said he was in the doghouse because he

Saved From The Fire?

couldn't find his black pants. No wonder neither of them attend church as adults or have found Jesus yet. Yes, we were all baptized as infants and my Father and Mother both were there. That was an act of our parent's faith we were unsure to follow.

If you read about baptism in the Bible, they dedicated babies to the Lord, no baptism. They practiced Believers baptism upon profession of faith.

My sister, Gretchen, the eldest of us five

siblings, got into a small group Bible study at another church and found a relationship with Jesus and met the Holy Spirit. She was a senior that year, and Dad thought she'd fallen into a cult or something. I was a daddy's girl and didn't want to be on his bad side, so I wasn't open to what my sister had, and she didn't feel free to share with me. She went away to college and I went into fourth grade.

My dad died suddenly January 1975, when I was in 6th grade. Mom said later she stopped praying when Dad died. I never knew she prayed. About the time I wanted a Sunday off because the choir had it off, Mom was going to church again and insisted I attend. This was a God intervention!

I will break in here to say that Mom had been part of churches most of her life and was a good, religious, work-oriented, Biblical values kind of Christian. She realized just before she died being born again was something she needed and didn't have. The hospital chaplain led her to Jesus the last

Musings Along Life's Journey
By Heidi Honey

time she was in the hospital. Her last couple weeks on Hospice she was at peace; her soul finally found rest from the works of religion and was satisfied.

I found Jesus when I was twenty years old.

Remember my eczema testimony? The eczema on

my hands began during this October move of my 20th year. The apartment we moved to was the first time in our married life we had cable T.V. and I watched **The 700 Club** for the first time. Ben Kinchlow prayed the prayer of Salvation at the end of each show. I prayed the sinner's prayer with him each day from Monday to Friday because I felt no change and wasn't sure I did it right. Ben mentioned on Friday he realized you might feel nothing when you pray for salvation. You had to take it by faith that you asked Jesus in and He came in! Hallelujah, I found Jesus as my savior!

A couple months later, Jehovah's Witnesses came to my door and offered free Bible study in my home. I jumped at the chance because I had two under two, and it was challenging to get out. Also, I had a cousin married to a Jehovah's Witness pastor's daughter who had helped him get off drugs in a half-way house. They worked at The Watchtower Society in New York City. Well, the older woman came with a book and their Bible. It wasn't long before my two-year-old eating breakfast at the table we were working on could repeat everything the woman was feeding us out of her book. I wondered why it

Saved From The Fire?

was so simple that my daughter could

understand. The woman taught us Jesus died on a stake; not a cross, you shouldn't have children because the end is coming and woe to those nursing and pregnant! Christmas and Easter were pagan celebrations... so many things I'd never known before! Did I mention I didn't read the Bible myself yet? My JW teacher made me fearful I wouldn't be saved without joining The Watchtower and the woman had invited me to their church for a sledding party. One day she stopped, I could see she was troubled seeing I was
noticeably pregnant with my third child and we were decorating the tree for Christmas.

    This was a strange time in my young life. We were only in that apartment for nine months. When we moved across town, I thought I'd lost my "Bible teacher." She found our new apartment. Before she did, I found an ad in the Adirondack Home Journal, a free weekly paper. "Are you involved with Jehovah's Witnesses? Do you want help? Do you want the truth?" I only saw that ad in the paper once, but I held on to it and called the number a couple weeks later. It connected me with a young mother named Cheryl. Her family had been part of Jehovah's Witnesses. She knew deep down it wasn't right and as they went two by two to witness, she would pray as they came to the door that no one would answer. God led her into truth. She gave me several cassette tapes talking about the abuses, false teachings, and the origins of the Jehovah's Witnesses. In God's way of showing His glory, I found later that Cheryl had been part of the church I now go to at the time I met her.

Musings Along Life's Journey
By Heidi Honey

In 1983, Reverend John Martin and his family pastored the Presbyterian church I attended. His wife joined our choir. During practice she asked, "So when do you have your Bible studies?" Bible Studies? Our church didn't have any of those! So, Reverend Martin started a Bible study. He began with the book of Revelation. As I began reading the Bible myself, I learned a lot. I had also learned a lot in my "home study" that took several years to sort out what was true, false, or didn't matter. That was three years before I encountered the Holy Spirit.

The Spirit of Poverty

We have all heard of monks and nuns taking a vow of poverty and giving everything to the church to devote themselves to a life of simplicity, prayer, and good works. Sounds like an idyll life to some:
being a good, humble Christian. Is this what Jesus has called His people to do?

I remember a couple who came to speak at our church; it must have been a decade or so ago! The husband said you have a spirit of poverty when you think you're too poor to go out and buy an ice cream cone. I understood. I have never known how much to charge people when I've done childcare in my home or cleaning and odd jobs for neighbors. I never thought we had enough to pay for things for our children's activities during their school years. I was taught a lot of fear about finances from my mother who grew up during the depression and my husband who grew up in a big family with little money.

On the other hand, I heard a testimony of a missionary family who lived way back in the boonies in a foreign country. There was a famine in the area, and no one had been out to see the family until the crisis was over. They thought the family would

be starved but found them healthy, the kids

rosy cheeked. They had feasted on the Word of God! Did you know the Bible has milk, bread, meat, and honey? The four types of Scripture and the levels of understanding you get as you read and meditate. This story truly shows what Jesus taught and King David spoke about in the Psalms.

Musings Along Life's Journey
By Heidi Honey

"But He answered and said, It is written, 'Man shall not live by bread alone, but by every word that proceeds from the mouth of God.'" (Matthew 4:4)

I have not departed from the commandment of His lips; I have treasured the words of His mouth More than my necessary food.
(Job 23:12)

Was Jesus Poor?

The Bible says Jesus became poor so we may become rich, but was Jesus really poor? Kat Kerr [www.revealingheaven.com] shares that Jesus was the son of a master carpenter here on earth. The gifts the Maggi brought Him were more riches than most people owned in a lifetime. If we think about it, why would a poor person need a treasurer to take care of his money? Note how Jesus knew who would betray Him but made Judas Iscariot one of His twelve closest disciples and put him in charge of His finances. Along with trust in God for everything He needed, I think this shows Jesus' mercy and grace to the utmost!

Would people invite a poor family to their wedding? The master carpenter made furniture and would have made special things for the bridal couple and been invited to the wedding. I have heard all

The Spirit of Poverty

Jesus' travels during His life on earth were within a two-hundred-mile radius. He was taught in Hebrew school as all good Jewish boys were and apprenticed to His earthly father, Joseph, but only used a vocabulary of 200 words. Compared to Heaven where He came down from, this was small stuff. Only a humble Savior would confine Himself to earthly parameters and stoop low to make a way for the ones He loves, conforming to the will of the Father. His purpose was to bridge the gap between Father God and His children.

He loves us all and longs to have a relationship with us. Our original father Adam's sin severed the relationship with Father God for all until Jesus came and sacrificed to return us to that original relationship Adam and Eve had, walking in the garden of Eden with Him. This was the joy set before Jesus that made it so He could endure the cross. God made humankind as siblings for Jesus and Jesus wanted to bring His family back to Father God.

The Bible is full of verses which ascribe richness in all aspects of life here on earth. God supplies all our needs according to His riches in Christ Jesus if we recognize that provision and let Him do it. We are to believe He provides and ask Him for what we need and want; just like your children do with you, or you do to your parents. Much of our struggle comes from not trusting God's promises or not appropriating them for ourselves and our families. Remember what I said about the meaning of Shalom? That's the fullness of God; the completeness He wants to shower on us, even this side of heaven.

Musings Along Life's Journey
By Heidi Honey

Putting Things in God's Hands

Jesus wants you to see that the devil owns the finances of this world. But when we give to God, we take our finances out of satan's hands and put them back into Kingdom use. Listening to Dr. Kevin Zadai and reading his book **Supernatural Finances**, I have been on a journey to see how finances work from God's perspective. Let me share some of this journey with you.

> *"Give, and it will be given to you: good measure, pressed down, shaken together, and running over will be put into your bosom. For with the same measure that you use, it will be measured back to you."*
> (Luke 6:38)

When I was starting to learn about giving and receiving, I would give in amounts of twenty or thirty dollars and funds would come back to me in twenty to fifty-dollar amounts. When I was bold and gave one hundred dollars, I got back funds in the hundred-dollar range. This was just a learning grace the Lord led me through because God does not always give back dollars for giving dollars. I have been tithing; giving a tenth of what comes my way, since I learned about tithing over thirty years ago. Not to be legalistic about it, but one tenth is an easy amount to figure! Seeing as how God gives you power to get wealth, it ultimately all belongs to Him anyway. So if we give back the first part, He blesses the rest. Do you know the devil owns the financial system?

The Spirit of Poverty

When we give to God first, the rest of our finances are taken out of the devil's hands!

Check out my 'Yellow Bananas' section to see testimonies of how the Lord blessed me as I gave and then provided for my needs in return for my
giving. Remember my story of the couple who visited our church and said you have a spirit of poverty if you think you can't afford an ice cream cone? That was a few years back and I thought I'd dealt with the spirit of poverty, but there's always more to learn!

Yes, I thought I was over the poverty mentality until an experience in January of 2020. I had saved funds from my seasonal work at the motel to pay for my needs through the winter. In January, I noticed the savings were beginning to dwindle. Right then, my boss at the motel texted me with a job offer cleaning for a friend's brother-in-law. I praised God for knowing just when I needed finances and began the job. The man asked what I get paid, and I said I got twelve dollars an hour at the motel. He said that was not enough. He wanted to pay me twenty- five! The first two weeks it took me three hours to clean his house when I thought it would only take two. When he offered me seventy-five, I talked him down to sixty dollars. Not just once, but twice!

Well, I had lunch with my good friend Cindy that week. She pointed out I had a spirit of poverty! She also reminded me that a workman is worth his wages. [1 Timothy 5:18] This immediately convicted me and I spent the next few days wondering how I would.

Musings Along Life's Journey
By Heidi Honey

tell the man I'd take the full amount after the two weeks I short-changed myself.

Glory! He didn't even ask how much that day, just asked if I'd take a check because he didn't have cash. He made the check out for seventy-five dollars! Later, my husband John told me if the man hired a cleaning service, they would charge twice as much as he's paying me. Perspective!

With the Covid-19 outbreak, I can still clean for him once a week and work at the motel. I've been enjoying the freedom to donate to what our church is doing to bless our communities during this time. I've also been able to give offerings over and above what I already give monthly to other organizations.

Having been part of short-term mission trips and a trip to Israel, I have had to trust God for finances. He has made it clear to me I cannot fret about the finances or try to make them up by myself. He is a good Father who is never early, never late, but right on time because He knows just when we need things.

Another testimony is how my husband has supported me and helped me raise money for the trips and blessed me as I have gone on them. Sometimes I dream about how much money the church would get if we tithed off our income instead of just what I get from my part-time jobs. John has been incredibly good to me, making sure I had some money to give to the church when I didn't have a job

The Spirit of Poverty

because he realizes people who go to church should have money to put in the offering plate. I know Glory days are ahead and my dreams shall be fulfilled!

Businesspeople

Even Caitlin Pyle who owns, **Proofread Anywhere,** and does not profess to be a Believer, says you need to change your mindset about money. You need to see money as a renewable resource instead of a finite one. Caitlin was interviewed by Eric Brotman on his **Don't Retire...Graduate** podcast where he interviews people like Caitlin who are making options available for older people to not 'retire and settle

for a fixed income'. He said, "A fixed income is not fixed, it's actually eroding." In other words, if you're on Social Security or a pension, you get a 'cost of living' increase, but it does not keep up with the true cost of living.

Going back to Kat Kerr, a businessperson like Caitlin, she's had revelation of God putting an entrepreneurial spirit into His people in these times. Believers are supposed to be starting businesses that take finances out of the hands of the wicked and put them back into the kingdom here on earth (as it is in heaven). Then, those we take the funds from become Believers!

So what business have you thought about starting? What skill do you have that other people need? Alexa Bigwarf of Kat Biggie Press in her book, **Ditch the Fear; Just Write It!** says, "I'm sure

Musings Along Life's Journey
By Heidi Honey

you've heard the statistics...more than 80% of the population wants to write a book. But guess what? Only less than 2% of people will

actually do it." Take some time to think about this and seek the Lord
about how you should implement your business plan. By the way, Alexa says if you publish a book, you have a business so learn how to promote and incorporate. Yes, this means a website! Be encouraged; there are lots of tutorials and options.

A Big Step

From listening to Kat and now learning from Alexa Bigwarf and Caitlin Pyle, I'm ready to begin my own freelance business. There's a bit of trepidation since I've never done something like this before, but with what I'm learning and Holy Spirit's prompting, I'm on my way! It will take time, work, and some finances. You may need some training. I'm getting mine from Caitlin, Alexa and Word Press tutorials. I suggest you check out Caitlin [https://www.Proofreadany- where.com] she has a good blog you can use to read about work-at-home scams before you get too deep into things!

By the way, join me in praying for Caitlin and Alexa. They are prospering financially with the business, books and courses each has created. But they both have a sore heart only Jesus can heal. I'd love to see their financial blessings blessing others for God, gaining them heavenly treasure for eternity and heart-peace here on earth. Pray for Caitlin's husband to come back; their marriage restored. Pray for healing for Alexa's family from the baby they lost.

We are to be pitied if we build up our own kingdoms and treasures here on earth and have nothing to take to heaven after the time we've spent here. Heavenly treasure does not get stolen, mold, rust or get moth eaten. Keep in mind:

How much better to get wisdom than gold! And to get understanding is to be chosen rather than silver.
(Proverbs 16:16)

Retire?

I do not plan to retire as the world plans. I plan to work while I am able, bringing the Word and will of God and His glory to as many as He gives me. I don't ever want to stop learning new things, especially from the Bible. In our house things are
shifting since my husband is retired, so I need something flexible, but he understands I want to do something business-like at this point. I want to be able to give more and to do more things for the kingdom. Kevin Zadai says, "The Gospel is free, but spreading it is costly." As many are saying, this epidemic has led unlikely

people to search for work-

Musings Along Life's Journey
By Heidi Honey

at-home options, even retirees. I end this topic with one final Scripture and something more to think about.

> *"I have shown you in every way, by laboring like this, that you must support the weak. And remember the words of the Lord Jesus, that He said, 'It is more blessed to give than to receive.'"* (Acts 20:35)

This Scripture has given me pause. Yes, it's great to be able to give to others! Getting something myself is nice, but so much more satisfying when I can give and help bless others. Just remember, the other person gets a reward for giving to or serving you. Don't steal their reward by being too proud to take what someone else wants to give you. In humility, I said to the senior citizens I worked with, "You've helped others for years. Now it's my turn to help you."

With A Voice Of Singing

I cannot remember a time I wasn't singing. Mom used to get us singing in the car as Dad drove and she sang lullabies every night from the time we were babies. Her mom sang often when we visited; all the old songs from the roaring 20's, before and beyond. I was in Junior Girl Scouts before I realized not everyone could sing when one of the girls told me she had a 'tin ear'.

I was part of chorus and church choir from the time I was in second grade. In sixth grade, our chorus teacher split us into parts for the first time. She apologized for putting me with the altos instead of sopranos. I was fine with that!

Singing Tenor

In seventh grade, because I could sing the Tenor part, I got to join the boys in the junior high chorus. I had been playing French horn for two years and was blessed with and developing a good ear for music, so I led the boys because most of them could sing if they got the first note, but not otherwise. I had tried to be a bit of a tomboy in elementary school, but that did not go well because I wasn't very tough and cried easily, so I wasn't trying to be that!

I got mixed reactions from the other tenors.

Musings Along Life's Journey
By Heidi Honey

Some were jealous of me; some didn't want a girl; especially me, in their group. The best singers tended to like having me part of their team because
I helped them get the first note and stay on the right line. I also was able to sing tenor in the adult choir at church. My Spanish teacher was also in the tenor section, but she wasn't as competent as my brash little self. The older men in the group were good mentors for me.

I need to mention here that I did not meet Jesus as my personal savior until I was 20 years old. I figured I attended church, sang in the choir, so I must be a Christian. I was known in school for being a 'goody-goody' or 'goody two shoes' and I didn't know it, but I was full of pride.

Mom would wonder where I got the low voice from. I found out her mother sang tenor in church when she was younger. There was a story of Grandma being sick with meningitis when she was fourteen. She was left in the hospital for the night without much hope. Her family knew she would live when they walked in the next morning to Della singing at the top of her lungs!

My senior year of high school, I was in an Area Allstate chorus and stood next to another female tenor. She either sang the alto part, or the soprano line an octave lower. What an eye opener for me!

With A Voice Of Singing

God made up for this twenty years later. I was in the Jefferson Singers at our community college in spring of 2000. My professor got information on a chance to sing in a Mid America Productions concert at Carnegie Hall. I jumped at the chance!

Big Adventure

Professor Scrivani-Tidd sent in application, and I was accepted. It meant I had to get a CD of Mozart's Requiem and the music to learn my parts and purchase a black formal dress to wear. In mid-January 2001, I had my first solo ride on a train from Utica, NY to Grand Central Station. Also my first solo ride in a taxi; I didn't realize how close my hotel was and I didn't communicate with the driver well. He got an excellent tip due to my naivete.

    My mom came and stayed in a room in the same hotel as me the next day, Trump Towers! That evening we walked together down the street and found a shoe store getting ready to close, but not before I could get a pair of shoes to go with the dress I bought. I roomed with a young lady that worked at Miss Vicky's/Victoria's Secret. We had some good conversations.

    Earlier that day we all walked from the hotel to our first practice session. What a treat to sit amid a bunch of tenors I didn't have to lead or help keep on key! They all had the music down pat; a little taste of heaven, I think (yes, I knew Jesus and Holy

Musings Along Life's Journey
By Heidi Honey

Spirit by this time). We had two more practices and a dress rehearsal where our mass choir stood and practiced with an orchestra and the soloists. I was in awe of Carnegie Hall since I'd heard about it all my life as the epitome of performance and never been in it before. It amazed me that the high school kids in the group from NYC area had performed there with their school groups! In Northern New York, the closest we got was Area All State or Bi-County events at the colleges.

The concert was amazing. I think I had a small taste of what Mozart heard in his head while he was composing the Requiem. What an experience! At the
end, we took a dinner cruise on the Hudson. Mom was able to come with us. She died four years later, so this trip was a great memory to store away. Also, I was working at Brookside Senior Living Community at that time. All the people there were part of this journey and so happy to share it with me. Sadly, the event was supposed to be taped and I should have gotten a copy of it to share, but it never materialized. I hope this is something I get to see in heaven and that many, if not all the people who supported and shared this experience will be there to see it also!

All This and Heaven Too!

As amazing as that experience was, it is nothing compared to the glory of heaven to come. It's like a dress rehearsal for the heavenly choir, but pale

With A Voice Of Singing

in comparison. I am thankful for the gift of

singing and the gift of music and all the training I have had over the years to develop these gifts. I don't ever want to lose the wonder I find in worshipping my Creator God in song. I never want to stop giving thanks. I remember when I was first at the Rhema Mennonite Fellowship church and part of a group of ladies that sang for our part of an ecumenical Good Friday service. Our Pastor introduced us as
'the musicians'. Of course, I'd heard that before, but when he said it, it clicked. I am God's musician. Not just a singer, not just a French horn player. As I see myself as a scribe for the Holy Spirit when I write, I see myself as a mouthpiece for the wind of the Spirit when I sing or play.

> *As each one has received a gift, minister it to one another, as good stewards of the manifold grace of God. If anyone speaks, let him speak as the oracles of God. If anyone ministers, let him do it as with the ability which God supplies, that in all things God may be glorified through Jesus Christ, to whom belong the glory and the dominion forever and ever. Amen.*
> (1 Peter 4:10-11)

Yellow Bananas

September 2, 2019, I watched Keith Ellis on YouTube. I became acquainted with him on Sid Roth's ISN. Keith saw a vision of yellow bananas. It was a big bunch. Keith prophesied yellow for gifts, a bunch meaning many gifts coming.

The Bible tells us it is good to give thanks to the Lord, and to sing praises to His name, so I accepted this word of prophecy and began writing down gifts and blessings I saw and giving thanks. I hope it gets you inspired to give thanks for what He puts in your life as well!

September 2-18

1. I won a painting...
   It's a really nice wooden frame with two children in a peaceful setting and Isaiah 32:18 "*My children will dwell in a peaceful habitation*" is inscribed on the frame at the bottom. Lord, bless the artist, the person who made the frame, and the one who donated the picture to benefit the library. Amen.

Musings Along Life's Journey
By Heidi Honey

2. Blessed with a scarf...
   I found a scarf under the bed when I cleaned the motel. It was a blessing to clean this messy room (they had several young children in that room for several days!) Lord, bless the family from Rochester who left the scarf. Amen.

3. Chocolate!
   We enjoyed dark chocolate almond squares left by a motel guest to bless us workers. Lord, bless that group of men. Amen.

4. Rug blessing...
   Got a $35.00 rug for $5.00 at Lowe's. We saw the clearance rack just in time; when we went back by a few minutes later, the rugs were all gone. Thanks Jesus, you knew just what I needed. It fits perfectly in front of the washer/dryer! Amen.

5. Financial Blessing...
   Blessed with two hour's pay and $40.00 tip; I was at church and didn't get text from boss; I showed up when she didn't think she needed any more help. Lord, thanks for rebuking the devourer. Amen.

6. Gift Bag...
   I missed Joy's last day at work; she left a gift bag for me with a soup mug and a wooden star that said "Home" on it. Lord, bless Joy's trip back to Florida. Amen.

7. Garage Sale gifts...
   My neighbor Paula sold me two baskets, one necklace, and four pair of earrings for $3.00. She had jewelry marked $1.00 each, baskets marked $3.00 each. Lord, bless Paula for

Yellow Bananas

blessing me. Amen.

8. Gift Card...
   John's sister Barb gave him the card; she found it in her purse and didn't know how much was on it. It was $15.00, that paid for half our breakfast. Lord, thank You for blessing us with a morning out together.

9. Black jacket...
   I was thinking I needed a new winter jacket. Barb gave me a jacket she couldn't wear. Just what I was wanting! Lord, bless Barb for her generosity and thank You for knowing my need before I asked. Amen.

September 20-24

1. Andrew and John Eastmond...
   Nataleigh's Ninth birthday was yesterday, she got to spend the night with me and attend this concert at our church [September 20, 2019]. This was when Andrew gave me the word about 'He has gone before me'. I was able to buy Natty one of Kathy's framed photos and John's new music CD. It was good seeing Andrew's wife Kathy and her photographs, as well as Andrew and John. Thank You Lord, for good friends and Spiritual blessings. Amen.

2. Pending over-draw...
   I have given all our finances to Jesus, laying them on an altar in my bedroom. When I saw

Musings Along Life's Journey
By Heidi Honey

this overdraw happening, I realized the cash from tip money [from the day I went in by
mistake] will cover it! Thank You Father, for providing. Amen.

3. Old Friends...
   Friends from Lowville came to my church looking for a new church. Thank You Lord, for the blessing of good

friends. Amen...

4. Prompt obeyed/felicitous bonus!
   The Holy Spirit inspired me to stop at the farm stand on way home from church. I only had $10.00 cash (no change) so I bought three bundles of "bulk" tomatoes to round out my canning and was gifted two Gladiola stalks for spending $10.00. Thank You Lord, for the beautiful flowers and that I was able to bless this neighbor and fill my canner. Amen.

5. Eastmond Poster...
   Janelle had an extra poster from the Eastmond concert. She knew Nataleigh really likes them and gave me the poster to give to her. Thank You Lord, for the Eastmond family encouraging this young one. Amen.

I forgot about this list and missed many gifts! I resumed recording in January of 2020.

January 26 – February 7, 2020

Yellow Bananas

1. Gift of encouragement...
I finally figured out how to view comments on

my blog. Lord, thanks for all the wonderful comments I was able to read today. They were so encouraging! Your fruit is evident that I am Your scribe; thanks that people are using my posts for Bible study! Amen.

1. Thankful Reflection...
   I was copying my pages to Word docs so I could begin this book. Thank You Lord, for taking me back to some things You showed me to write months ago. What a gift! Amen.

2. **Acres Of Diamonds**...
   I get a free book for being part of Jentezen Franklin's book launch! Thank You Lord, for letting me be part of this team. The book is so encouraging!

February to Juneteenth

I began another page with February 10th and 12th. I have included one from April, May and June. Notice I slowed down on my recording; no condemnation taken!

1. No sound...
   It was good to work out without sound. It's a real gift to talk through the whole workout, especially since Pahla doesn't drink any water

Musings Along Life's Journey
By Heidi Honey

on the video! Lord, bless my 'virtual' friend Pahla and let me meet her in heaven someday. Amen.

2. Blessed Mike & Rose's family...

   It was a blessing to watch the house, get their little girl off the bus, pick up the house and pray for peace in the chaos, salvation over household, sang Jesus songs to the little girl while she rested. Father, thanks for the chance to minister and sow seeds in this precious family. Amen.

3. Old fleece/New vest...
   Thank You Lord, for John giving me the idea to cut the sleeves off the old fleece I bought at the thrift store. It's just what I needed working, spring-cleaning motel rooms in this chilly weather. Amen.

4. Blessed to be blessed...
   I was able to help Chris and Jenn pack up the house, clean, and take care of what was left. I was blessed with several things we can use, including an under-bed storage box. Lord, bless them in their new home. Amen.

5. Another free book!

I get to be on the launch team for Rick Renner's new book **Last Days Survival Guide**. Its premier is August 2nd, 2020. Father,

Yellow Bananas

thank You for this opportunity to help promote what Your Spirit is teaching. Amen.

As I said earlier, this is just a sampling of what I saw the Lord doing. God is working all the time, blessing us so we can be a blessing to others. In Vacation Bible School, it was the kids' favorite time when we asked them to tell us their 'God Sightings', what they saw God do in their life that day. If one talked about a rainbow, the others would talk about seeing the rainbow. Father God doesn't mind if each of us thanks Him for the same thing; we all see it differently!

I hope this has opened your thoughts to be on the lookout for what God is doing in and around you every day.

Conclusion

In conclusion, I hope I have inspired you to see what good things are happening in your life amidst the chaos and heartache. Have I spurred you on to pursue a deeper relationship with Jesus the Son, Holy Spirit and Father God? Have you had a revelation sparked from me sharing my testimonies? God says this life is just a vapor, a drop in the bucket. Are you spending your life well? I am here if you have any questions and look forward to my next book, where I will share more of my adventures from this journey of life.

One of our fathers of the faith has said, "Good hymnody is good theology." With this thought, I leave you with the words of a hymn that came to me this morning. Yes, I am thankful for God's compassions and new mercies each morning. I see His hand in the manifold witness of nature, manifesting His faith- fulness, mercy, and love. What would I do without His pardon for sin and overwhelming peace, His presence giving guidance, strength for today, and bright hope for tomorrow? This hymn combines so many truths of God as my Father, it has imparted a lot of truth and wisdom for my life. Join me in extoling His manifest grace!

Musings Along Life's Journey
By Heidi Honey
Great Is Thy Faithfulness

1. Great is thy faithfulness, O God my Father, there is no shadow of turning with thee.
   Thou changest not, thy compassions, they fail not; as thou hast been, thou forever wilt be.

Refrain:

Great is thy
faithfulness! Great
is thy faithfulness!
Morning by morning new mercies I
see; all I have needed thy hand hath
provided. Great is thy faithfulness,
Lord, unto me!

2. Summer and winter and springtime and harvest, sun, moon, and stars in their courses above
   join with all nature in manifold witness to thy great faithfulness, mercy, and love.

   [Refrain]

3. Pardon for sin and a peace that endureth, thine own dear presence to cheer and to guide, strength for today and bright hope for tomorrow, Blessings all mine, with ten thousand beside!

[Refrain]

Source: Christian Worship (2021): Hymnal #602
Library.timlesstruth.org

Author Heidi Honey

Photograph By
Jennifer L. Honey

What Drives My Writing?

I have been writing since about fourth grade when I spelled very 'verry' and Dad said he knew what I wrote about was extreme, but very only has one 'r'!

My journaling began sporadically when I became a Believer, pouring my heart out about what was going on in my life, writing short songs, and recording what the Lord was doing in my life. Each year I have journaled more as I discover new things or nuances of things I thought I understood. This led to the Lord prompting me to start a blog, which morphed into His prompting me to publish my first book.

The events and stories in this book are some highlights of my life that the Lord brought forth to share with others as I take time to muse/meditate, bringing clarity. The things I've included answer questions others have asked me about what I've discovered. I hope my readers find encouragement and new understanding of what it means to journey with the God of the universe who cares about each soul He created. It is not about religion or which church you go to, it's about a personal relationship with Jesus, who restored our relationship with Father God.

To order more copies of this book, contact Amazon. A signed copy of the first edition can be obtained by request.
 email: heidi.e.honey@gmail.com

Zoe Life Christian Communications

WORDS TO LIVE BY

Made in the USA
Columbia, SC
27 November 2023

e143933f-a2d0-4557-bde3-cc8a91830e7eR01